First Look at . . .
dBASE IV
Version 1.5/2.0 for DOS

First Look at . . .
dBASE IV
Version 1.5/2.0 for DOS

Wilson Price

Mitchell McGRAW-HILL

New York St. Louis San Francisco Auckland Bogotá Caracas
Lisbon London Madrid Mexico Milan Montreal New Delhi Paris
San Juan Singapore Sydney Tokyo Toronto Watsonville

To some special people in my life:

Emmi, Janice, and Linda.

Mitchell **McGRAW-HILL**
Watsonville, CA 95076

First Look at dBASE IV Version 1.5/2.0 for DOS

2 3 4 5 6 7 8 9 0 DOH DOH 9 0 9 8 7 6 5 4

ISBN 0-07-051075-X

Sponsoring editor: Erika Berg
Editorial assistant: Jennifer Gilliland
Technical reviewer: Mark Workman, Frank Phillips College
Director of production: Jane Somers
Production supervisor: Leslie Austin
Project manager: Carol Dondrea, Bookman Productions
Interior designer: Renee Deprey
Compositor: Bookman Productions
Cover designer: Janet Bollow
Cover photo: W. Warren/**West**light
Printer and binder: R. R. Donnelley & Sons

Library of Congress Card Catalog No. 93-79559

Contents

LESSON 4

Creating and Using Forms

LESSON 5

Indexing and Searching Data Files

Preface to the Instructor

First Look at dBASE IV Version 1.5/2.0 for DOS is a self-paced, hands-on tutorial which covers the essential and most commonly used features of dBASE IV. This book can be used:

- in a short course on dBASE IV Version 1.5 or 2.0
- as a supplement in a microcomputer applications course
- as a supplement in a variety of business courses
- as a self-paced guide to dBASE IV

Written in plain, simple English using step-by-step instructions, this book and other books in the First Look Series quickly get the reader "up to speed" with today's popular software packages in a minimum number of pages. Complete with a Command Summary, a helpful Troubleshooting Guide, and a thorough Index, *First Look at dBASE IV Version 1.5/2.0 for DOS* makes reference quick and easy.

ORGANIZATION

First Look at dBASE IV Version 1.5/2.0 for DOS begins with basic start-up information, then progresses to more advanced features of dBASE IV. These features aid learning in each lesson:

- **Objectives** provide an overview
- **Step-by-step, hands-on tutorials** guide the reader through specific functions and commands
- **Screen displays** monitor the reader's progress
- **Summary of Commands** makes reference quick and easy
- **Review Questions** reinforce key concepts
- **Hands-on Exercises** require readers to apply the skills and concepts just learned

As readers work through *First Look at dBASE IV Version 1.5/2.0 for DOS*, they create files that are used in later lessons. These files should be saved on a data disk so they can be easily located and retrieved. It is assumed that readers have access to the full-powered software package and all its features.

Use the First Look Series for brief and affordable coverage of today's most popular software applications packages.

. . . .
ACKNOWLEDGMENTS

I wish to thank the following people who provided excellent comments in their reviews:

Desmund Chun, Chabot College

Terry Cooper, Medicine Hat College

Curtis Meadow, University of Maine

Pam Nelson, Panhandle State University

Robert Norton, San Diego Mesa College

Linda Price, NASA

Mark Workman, Frank Phillips College

Marilyn Zook, Mt. Hood Community College

                                                    Wilson Price

Getting Started

ÓBJECTIVES

In this lesson you will learn how to:

- Bring dBASE IV up on the computer.
- Negotiate around the dBASE menu system.
- Obtain help in the form of on-screen descriptions of various dBASE actions.
- Terminate a dBASE session.

TRYING DBASE

Keyboard Nomenclature

Directions for you to follow in this book frequently refer to keys of the keyboard. For instance, the Shift key is designated by Shift, and the Escape key by Esc. The Enter key Enter is identified on some computers as the Return key; in on-screen dBASE menus this key is indicated by a bent arrow ←.

In many cases you use combinations of keys. This should be familiar to you from holding down Shift while typing a letter key to get uppercase. Whenever you are to use such a key combination, this book will show both keys separated by a hyphen. For instance, Alt-F3 means *Hold down* Alt *and press* F3, *then release* Alt. Note that *press* means to tap the key lightly (as though you were typing); do not hold it down because keys on the computer keyboard automatically repeat (except for Shift, Ctrl, Alt, and a few others).

Controlling dBASE from the Control Center

You control the actions of dBASE IV with special dBASE **commands**. Each command directs the computer to do something. There are two ways you can control dBASE IV interactively, that is, execute the commands from the keyboard. The first way is from the dot prompt. Under control of the dot prompt, dBASE displays a dot (period) on the screen and positions the cursor immediately following it.

Many people find the dot prompt difficult to use, because it is easy to forget or confuse commands if you use dBASE infrequently. To get around this problem, dBASE IV includes a special feature called the **Control Center**, shown in Figure 1-1, which allows you to perform all the dBASE commands from a menu system.

Figure 1-1
The Control Center
screen

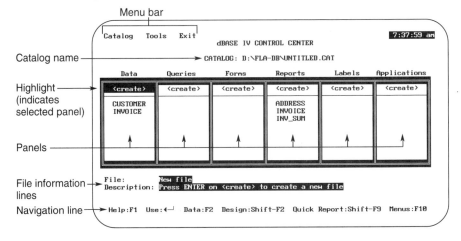

As labeled, the Control Center consists of five basic elements. The **menu bar** provides useful tools for managing files and changing the dBASE setup. You will experiment with the menu bar later in this lesson.

The **catalog line** designates the disk drive and subdirectory you are working in as well as the current dBASE catalog. A **catalog** is a collection of files that are handled as a group. You will learn about catalogs in Lesson 2.

The center portion of the screen consists of six **panels** that display the defined elements of your database system that are available to you. For instance, the Control Center in Figure 1-1 shows, in the **Data** panel, that two data files (CUSTOMER and INVOICE) have been set up and are available. Similarly, three different reports have been defined (ADDRESS, INVOICE, and INV_SUM) as listed in the **Reports** panel.

The two **file information lines** list the name and description of the file highlighted in the panel section. Because the highlight is on <create> the display is *New file*.

The **navigation line** shows which keys accomplish appropriate dBASE functions from the Control Center. The display on this line depends upon where you are in the Control Center menu system.

In addition, you will sometimes see below the navigation line a message line, giving you more information about particular options.

Experimenting with the Control Panel

In order to use the Control Panel, you first have to start dBASE IV. The steps to take depend upon your particular installation. For instance, in a school environment where many computers are linked together on a network, the startup sequence may be unlike anything you would find with an independent personal computer. In most cases, however, you begin dBASE by simply typing the command **DBASE** and pressing Enter in response to the operating system prompt. After a few moments, the dBASE Control Center screen (Figure 1-1) should be displayed. If instead of this screen a dot prompt with a flashing cursor next to it is displayed, type the command **ASSIST** and press Enter.

Unless your instructor has set up a special data disk for you (or you are working with the dBASE IV example files) your Control Panel display will not list any names in the panels. However, in Lesson 2 you will create your own entries. For now, experiment from the Control Center.

1. Press → four times.

   Notice that each time you press the key, the highlight moves to the next panel; in this case, it ends up on *<create>* in the Labels panel. If you were preparing to print address labels, you would work from this panel.

2. Press → two more times.

   Notice that after reaching the Applications panel, the highlight jumps back to the beginning (the Data panel). Needless to say, you could have returned to the Data panel by pressing ← repeatedly.

3. Look at the navigation line (bottom of the screen). The first entry is *Help:F1*. This tells you that to obtain help, you press F1 (a function key). Make sure that the highlight is in the Data panel and press F1.

   This produces the Help screen shown in Figure 1-2, which tells you all about creating database files.

4. Press F4 one or more times to move down successive screens through the continuous text description; press F3 to move backward in the text.

Figure 1-2
A Help screen

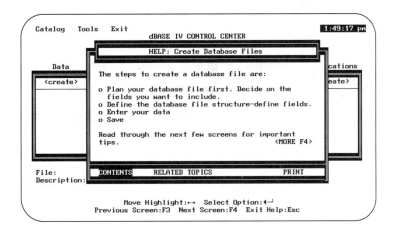

5. If you want to explore other topics related to creating database files, move the highlight to the *RELATED TOPICS* option. Then press Enter (as indicated by *Select Option:* ◄┘ on the navigation line) and your screen will display help information on another topic.

6. Feel free to explore the Help feature. When finished, press Esc to exit Help and return to the Control Center.

In this exercise, you called for Help when the highlight was in the Data panel. Had the highlight been in the Queries panel, for instance, the help descriptions would have told you about creating queries.

Menus from the Control Panel

The top line in Figure 1-1 is the **menu bar,** which is simply a list of options displayed side by side. The F10 function key gives you access to menus in dBASE, as the navigation line indicates with the message *Menus:F10.* Experiment with these features.

1. Press F10

The *Catalog* option of the menu bar is highlighted. A portion of the Control Center is overlaid with another menu, as shown in Figure 1-3. A menu of this type is called a **pull-down menu** because it is "pulled down" from the selected entry of the menu bar. Notice that the first entry of the pull-down menu, *Use a different catalog,* is highlighted.

Figure 1-3
The *Catalog* menu

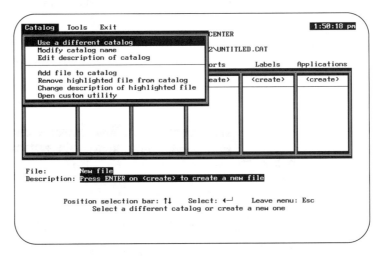

2. Suppose you wanted to select the *Add file to catalog* option. Press ↓ to move the highlight to the selected option and press Enter.

Another list of options is displayed to the right of the *Catalog* menu. This type of list is called a **pop-up menu** because it seemingly pops up out of nowhere.

3. Since you do not want to pursue this action, press (Esc) to get rid of the pop-up menu.

4. Press (Esc) again to get rid of the *Catalog* menu and return to the Control Center.

5. Now try the Design option on the navigation line. Press (Shift)-(F2) (remember: hold down (Shift), press (F2), then release (Shift)).

    This brings up an entirely different screen, one that allows you to define a database file, which you will do in the next lesson.

6. Press (Esc) to abort this action.

    When you do, dBASE displays a message box that says

    Are you sure you want to abandon operation?

    and provides you *Yes* and *No* options.

7. Notice that *No* is highlighted; it is the **default**. That is, by pressing (Enter), you do not confirm that you want to terminate the operation, so you remain in the file design screen. Try it by pressing (Enter)

8. Press (Esc) again and respond with (Y) (for "Yes, I want to abandon the operation").

    You are returned to the Control Center.

Terminating a dBASE Session

When you have completed a dBASE session, you should exit dBASE before turning off the computer. You do this from the Command Center through the menu bar.

1. Press (F10)

2. Press (→) twice to move the menu bar highlight to *Exit*.

    The pull-down menu shown in Figure 1-4 is displayed with *Exit to dot prompt* highlighted.

Figure 1-4
The *Exit* menu

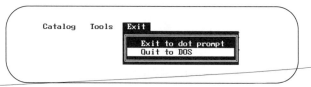

3. Move the highlight to the *Quit to DOS* option and press Enter

If you end up at the dot prompt, simply type **QUIT** and press Enter

In lessons that follow, you will encounter instructions telling you to select dBASE menu options. For instance, to terminate dBASE you will be told "from the Command Center select *Exit/Quit to DOS*" or simply "select *Exit/Quit to DOS*". Note that this implies that you must access the menu with F10, select *Exit*, then select *Quit to DOS* (as described in the preceding steps). Alternately, you may use either of the methods described in the next section.

Other Ways to Select Menu Options

Pressing F10 is one way to access a menu bar option from dBASE. Another way is with Alt plus the first letter of a command. For instance, to access the *Exit* menu use Alt-E; to access the *Catalog* menu use Alt-C. If you have a mouse connected to your computer, simply position the mouse pointer on the desired menu selection and click. In lessons that follow, when you are directed to access a menu entry, use whichever of these methods you prefer.

From the pull-down menu in Figure 1-4 you selected the *Quit to DOS* option by highlighting it and pressing Enter. Once in a pull-down or pop-up menu, there is another way: You can type the first letter of the option. For instance, you could simply press Q. (In some pop-up menus, several options may have the same first letter, in which case this method would not be practical.) If you have a mouse, position the mouse pointer on the desired menu option and click. Again, use whichever method you find most convenient.

About Intimidation

Beginning students commonly fear that pressing the wrong key will lead to disaster and destroy everything: all their work, perhaps themselves, the computer, and even the entire computer center. Be assured that this won't happen! (Perhaps I should say "shouldn't happen.") A keystroke that will have dire consequences is almost always accompanied by a warning. If you find yourself off on a tangent in some menu that you don't want, pressing Esc one or more times will usually get you out. It is interesting to note that children learn to use computers very quickly. Part of the reason is because they approach it with no built-in fears about what will happen if they do something wrong. So don't be intimidated!

■ *SUMMARY OF COMMANDS*

Most of the command sequences in this chapter are in the "try this" category. You will learn about their specific uses in later lessons. Commands to remember from this lesson are the following:

Topic or Feature	Command Sequence or Key	Page
Access a menu bar	F10	4
Abort an operation	Esc	6
Help	F1	3
Terminate a dBASE session	*Exit / Quit to DOS*	5

■ REVIEW QUESTIONS

1. What does the representation Shift-F2 mean?

2. You can carry out dBASE commands from the keyboard either from the _____ or the _____.

3. What are the five basic elements of the Control Center?

4. How can you get descriptive on-screen information that tells you about dBASE actions?

5. What key gives you access to dBASE menus?

6. If you have accidentally gone astray in the menu system and want to get back to the Control Center, which key would you press?

7. What single keystroke can destroy everything you have done?

Creating and Using Data Files

OBJECTIVES

In this lesson you will learn how to:

- Distinguish between numeric, character, date, and logical data.
- Create a data file.
- Enter data into a file.
- Edit existing data in a file.
- Obtain printed output for both a data file structure and records stored in the file.

COMPUTER DATA AND DATA TYPES

Organization of Data

One of the data files you will be working with is a collection of records on the customers of a business organization. When working with data files, you deal with three important entities: fields, records, and files. These basic units are illustrated in Figure 2-1. The following summarizes these terms.

Field	A basic unit of data (such as company name or address)
Record	A group of related facts or fields treated as a unit
File	The organized collection of all records of a given type

Figure 2-1
Field, record, and file

If you give some thought to the type of data you might want to store in a computer, two types come to mind: *alphabetic* and *numeric*. For instance, in a customer charge-account database file you would probably find a field for a customer name (alphabetic) and field for the amount owed on the charge account (numeric). Actually, dBASE includes six data classifications: character, numeric, float, date, logical, and memo.

Character Data Type

Many data items to be processed comprise letters, digits, and even special characters—that is, they consist of any of the characters on the keyboard. For example, a person's name may consist only of letters (Smith) or it may consist of letters and a digit (John Smith, 3rd). A Social Security number may be entered into the computer with the digits separated by hyphens, for example 123-45-6789. A purchase order number may include a letter as well as digits, for instance, 12275A. Information of this type is commonly called *character data*, or *string data*. The dBASE **character data type** allows for the storage of character data. However, a field need not include letters or special characters. For instance, a student number consisting of only digits might be defined as a character field. Here the field is a number, but one that will not be involved in arithmetic operations. (For instance, two student numbers would never be added together.) Because of the way in which numeric data is handled internally by the computer, the general practice is to define such fields as character, rather than numeric. When a character field is defined in a data file, its width (number of characters) must also be defined.

Numeric Data Type

Numeric data is data that can be used in arithmetic operations. This type consists of digits, which can be preceded by a plus or minus sign and which can include a decimal point. In defining the width of a numeric field, provisions must be made for a sign and/or a decimal point if they are to be included. For instance, consider three examples of numeric fields: student exam scores that range from 0 to 200, student grade point averages that range from 0.00 to 4.00, and a budget balance entry that can range from −500.00 to 500.00. Field requirements for each of these is illustrated in Figure 2-2.

Float Data Type

In addition, dBASE includes a special numeric data type called **float fields**, which provide for the storage of numbers in floating point form. This facilitates the handling of very large and very small numbers commonly used in scientific calculations. Float fields are not used in this book.

Figure 2-2
Typical numeric and
date data in memory

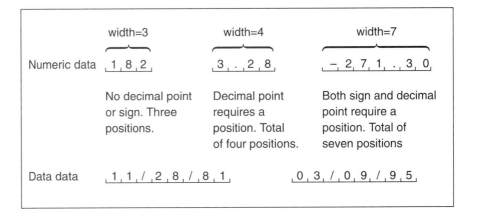

Date Data Type

A database often includes one or more **date fields**. For instance, an invoice might include both the date an order was placed and the date it was paid. The common format for representing dates is month/day/year. For example, November 28, 1994 is represented as 11/28/94; this is the format in which dBASE displays dates and allows you to enter them. Thus date fields are automatically allocated 8 positions when they are defined in a database file (refer to Figure 2-2).

Logical Data Type

Another common information storage need is to store Yes/No type of data—that is, data that answers such questions as "Is a student eligible for special benefits?" and "Is a customer eligible for a gold account?" In general, data such as this that can assume two different values (Yes/No or True/False) is called **logical data**. It is so common in computerized data processing that many conventional programming languages and almost all database systems provide the logical data type.

NOTE: Data of this type can also be stored in a single-character field where a given value such as "Y" means yes and some other value means no.

Memo Data Type

The memo data type is used for storing blocks of text information, or memo data. Sometimes a memo block is quite large, up to 5,000 characters. For each memo field in a database file, dBASE creates a separate memo file to store the memo data. The memo data type is not used in this book.

. . . .
DEFINING A NEW DBASE FILE

Example Definition

Assume you work for a consulting company that has contracts with numerous small businesses. You have been assigned the task of setting up a customer database file containing the following information.

Number	Field	Field Name	Type	Width	Decimals
1	Customer company name	COMPANY	Character	17	
2	Street address	ADDRESS	Character	17	
3	City	CITY	Character	10	
4	ZIP code	ZIP	Character	5	
5	Tax exemption status	EX	Logical	1	
6	Date of last order	LAST_ORD	Date	8	
7	Current account balance	BALANCE	Numeric	7	2

Field Width

Before you sit down to the computer to create a database file, you must do considerable planning. You must first determine all of the fields you will need and their types. In addition, you need to decide how many positions each character and numeric field will require (the field width). For some fields the width is predetermined by the field itself. For instance, state abbreviations are all two letters; thus the field width for a state field would be 2.

On the other hand, the field widths for company name and street address must be selected based on your knowledge of the data. These fields should be long enough to avoid chopping off the last few letters but not so long that they become clumsy to work with and waste computer storage space. Numeric fields must be long enough to hold the largest number that will be stored in them.

Character field widths in the customer file example are smaller than would normally be needed. These small values were chosen to simplify displaying the records on your computer screen for this example.

Field Names

Each field you define in a record must be given a **field name**. The choice is up to you, subject to the following restrictions.

- Names can be 1 to 10 characters in length and can contain letters, digits, and the underscore character.
- The first character must be a letter.
- The name cannot contain any blanks.

Do not confuse the name of a field with its contents. The name is the means by which you refer to a field that contains data you have entered. You should select names that are descriptive and suggest the contents of the field. Notice in the example definition LAST_ORD. An underscore is used to clarify; LASTORD might be confusing. On the other hand, notice that the Tax exemption status uses the short name EX; the word EXEMPT would be much more descriptive. (Similarly, LAST_ORDER could be used in place of LAST_ORD.) In both cases, the shorter names were selected solely to simplify displaying the file contents for this example.

Defining the Record Format in dBASE

With this background, you can proceed with defining the customer database file. As you make your entries, be aware that you can correct simple errors using the following keys.

Backspace	Delete the character to the left of the cursor.
Delete	Delete the character at the cursor.
↑, ↓, →, ←	Move up, down, left, and right to position the cursor on any character you want to change.

To begin, access dBASE; if your screen is at the dot prompt, type **ASSIST** and press Enter. You will be at the dBASE Control Center as shown in Figure 1-1 of the preceding lesson; the highlight will be positioned on *<create>* in the Data panel. Proceed as follows.

1. Press Enter

   The file design screen shown in Figure 2-3 is displayed. Note that the first line is highlighted, allowing you to define the first field of the file. The cursor is positioned at the beginning of the *Field Name* column.

2. Remember from Lesson 1 that you can get help by pressing F1. Do so and you will see a short description. When you are finished, Esc returns you to the file design screen.

3. Type **COMPANY** as the name of the first field in this database file, then press Enter

   The cursor jumps to the *Field Type* column where *Character* is already displayed. Character is the default data type.

4. Because COMPANY data will be the character type, accept the default by pressing Enter

Figure 2-3

Screen to define a
data file

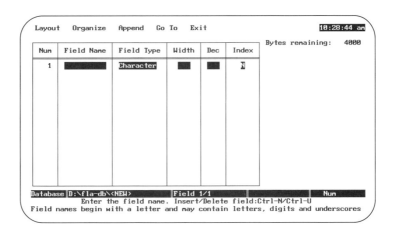

The cursor moves to the *Width* column.

5. Type **17** to enter the width value of the COMPANY field, then press
   [Enter]

   Notice that the 17 jumped to the right in this column and the cursor
   moved to the *Index* column, skipping the *Dec* column. The *Dec* column
   applies only to numeric fields, as you will soon see.

6. You need not be concerned with indexes for now, so press [Enter]

   The highlight moves down one line to field number 2.

7. Enter each of the fields **ADDRESS**, **CITY**, and **ZIP** with widths of **17**,
   10, and **5**, respectively, in exactly the same way you did for COMPANY.

   Remember, they are all character fields.

8. At field number 5 (Tax exemption status) type **EX** for the field name.

   Because EX is a logical field, not character, you must specify this.

9. Type the letter **L** (for logical), and the word *Logical* is displayed in the
   Field Type column.

   Notice that a value of 1 is entered automatically for the *Width* and that
   the cursor moves to the *Index* column. Press [Enter] to move to the next
   line.

10. For field number 6, type **LAST_ORD** as the field name.

    Be sure to use [Shift] for the underscore, otherwise you will get a hyphen,
    which is not valid for a field name.

11. Type **D** (for date).

    Notice that a width of 8 is entered automatically. Press [Enter]

12. For the last field, type **BALANCE** and select *Numeric* as the field type
    by typing **N**. Type **7** for the field width.

Because this is a numeric field, the cursor moves to the *Dec* column. Here you must enter the number of digits to the right of the decimal point. For a dollar-and-cent amount, the value is 2.

13. Type **2** for Dec. Then press [Enter] for no index.

This completes the record definition for this file; your screen should look like Figure 2-4. Check your screen carefully. If you see an error, move the cursor to the incorrect entry and change it.

Figure 2-4
The completed
record definition

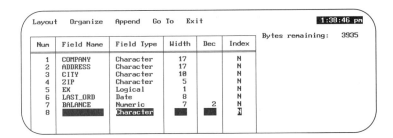

Num	Field Name	Field Type	Width	Dec	Index
1	COMPANY	Character	17		N
2	ADDRESS	Character	17		N
3	CITY	Character	10		N
4	ZIP	Character	5		N
5	EX	Logical	1		N
6	LAST_ORD	Date	8		N
7	BALANCE	Numeric	7	2	N
8		Character			N

14. To save your newly created file structure, select *Layout / Save this database file structure*. Remember from Lesson 1: Access the menu bar with [F10], make certain the highlight is on *Layout*, move the highlight to *Save this database file structure* of the pulldown menu, and press [Enter]

dBASE responds with the prompt *Save as*. At this point you must enter a filename for the database file. Since it is a DOS name, it must be eight or fewer characters.

15. Type **CUSTOMER** and press [Enter]

NOTE: If you are working on a network, follow file-naming rules established by your installation (if any).

16. To obtain a printed copy of your file structure, select *Layout / Print database structure*. From the resulting pop-up menu, select *Begin printing*.

17. When printing is completed, select *Exit / Save changes and exit*.

You will be returned to the Control Center.

This exercise has created a new database file on disk with the DOS filename and extension CUSTOMER.DBF (or whatever filename you used). The DBF (meaning Database File) is the dBASE default extension for database files and is added by dBASE automatically. Inspect the Control Center screen and you will see that your file is now listed in the Data panel. The file includes the complete record description as you have entered it but it does not include any records.

If you want to terminate your dBASE session, select *Exit / Quit to DOS*.

Entering Data

In a real business environment, you are usually adding, deleting, and changing records in a database file on a regular basis. To simulate this activity, you will enter the 16 records shown in Figure 2-5 in three separate sessions using two different data display screens.

Figure 2-5

Records for the customer file

```
Record  COMPANY         ADDRESS           CITY        ZIP     EX   LAST_ORD   BALANCE
  1     JP Designs, Inc. 1170 Burnett Ave. Concord     94520   N    07/06/93     0.00
  2     E Z Insurance   1443 West Q St.    Walnut      94457   N    08/15/93   221.50
  3     Municipal Utility 634 East Main St. Walnut     94596   Y    08/01/93   152.54
  4     Moraga Library  442 Euclid Avenue  Moraga      94561   Y                 0.00
  5     Pacheco Auto    155 Village Lane   Alamo       94573   N    07/05/93   355.34
  6     Arnold Hot Tub  118 Kellogg Way    Concordia   94522   N    08/09/93   803.00
  7     Eagle Book Store 1441 Q Street     Orinda      94563   N    08/14/93   221.38
  8     Union Fire Dept. 125 Churchill Sq. Union City  94533   Y    08/15/93     1.60
  9     Freiz Landscape 122 Loop Way       Rheem       94662   N    07/25/93   488.08
 10     Beverage Board  122 Central Way    Hap Hollow  94661   Y    08/01/93   642.15
 11     Board of Ed.    1 First Street     Hap Hollow  94661   Y    08/16/93   250.91
 12     Baker Pool Serv. 115 Center St.    Walnut      94569   N    08/06/93     0.00
 13     Coiffeur Hut    23 Orinda Way      Orinda      94563   N    08/05/93     0.00
 14     CC Social Serv. 123 Jackson Ave    Walnut      94572   Y    07/14/93   725.88
 15     Ramo's Tacos    155 Central Way    Alamo       94571   N                 0.00
 16     Carlson Metal   155 Industrial     Concord     94520   N    08/04/93    10.00
```

1. If you terminated the previous session, access dBASE.

   The Control Center now lists CUSTOMER in the Data panel as shown in Figure 2-6. Move the highlight to CUSTOMER (if it is not already there).

Figure 2-6

The Control Center with CUSTOMER

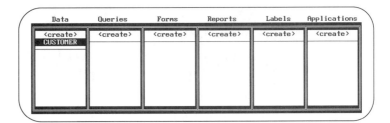

2. Refer to the navigation line at the bottom of the screen for a list of actions you can take. Select *Data:F2*, which allows you to append new records. Press F2

   The edit screen shown in Figure 2-7 appears, with the cursor located at the first position of the COMPANY field.

3. Enter the name of the first company, **JP Designs, Inc.**, and press Enter. The cursor jumps to the next line.

Figure 2-7
The data edit screen

4. Enter the ADDRESS and CITY fields for this record.

5. Next enter the five-digit ZIP code, which will fill the entire width of the ZIP field.

   When you type the last character (the 0), the cursor automatically progresses to the EX field, so do not press [Enter] or the cursor will skip to the LAST_ORD field.

   Remember that the Tax exemption status field (EX) is a logical field. You can enter Y or N for Yes or No, or you can enter T or F for True or False.

6. Because JP Designs, Inc. is not tax exempt (see Figure 2-5), type **N**.

   NOTE: dBASE makes the entry in uppercase letters even if you use lowercase.

7. Type the date **07/06/93**, including the leading zeros.

   Notice that you need not type the slash characters as they are already on the screen and the cursor jumps over them as you enter the digits. When the date entry is completed, the cursor jumps to the BALANCE field.

   Before entering the balance you might wish to check the fields already typed. If any are incorrect, move the cursor with the arrow keys and make your corrections. Remember, [Backspace] and [Delete] erase text.

8. The balance for JP Designs, Inc. is 0, so just press [Enter]

   Notice that you do not need to type the entire number 0000.00. The entries for the first record will be cleared from the screen.

9. For the second record (E Z Insurance) type the values for the first five fields, which will bring you to the LAST_ORD field.

10. To illustrate the internal checking done by dBASE, type the date as **18/15/93**.

    The computer beeps and the message

    Invalid date (press SPACE)

    appears at the bottom of the screen.

11. Press [Spacebar], and the cursor is repositioned to the date field at which point you can type in the correct value.

12. If necessary, press ⌈Enter⌉ to complete this field.

    The cursor moves to the BALANCE field.

13. Type **221**, the dollar amount for this record.

    Notice the blank space between the 1 and the decimal point.

14. Press ⌈.⌉, indicating a decimal point.

    Notice that the dollar amount is immediately positioned next to the decimal point.

15. Now type **50**.

    The record is saved and the edit screen goes blank.

16. Enter the next three records (Municipal Utility, Moraga Library, and Pacheco Auto) in the same way you entered the previous two.

17. Terminate data entry by accessing the menu bar and selecting *Exit/Exit*. You are returned to the Control Center.

Appending Additional Records to a File

You resume data entry into the CUSTOMER database as follows.

1. With the highlight on CUSTOMER in the Data panel of the Control Center press ⌈F2⌉

2. If the resulting screen displays each record on a single line, press ⌈F2⌉ again to get the edit screen (Figure 2-7).

    If you entered the records correctly, the record displayed should be the last one you entered: Pacheco Auto. Notice the status bar at the bottom of the screen. It includes the name of your data file *CUSTOMER* and the indication *Rec 5/5*. This means that the displayed record is the fifth of 5 records in the file.

    At this point, you need a menu to tell dBASE you want to add new records.

3. Access the *Records* menu (Figure 2-8) and select the *Add records* option.

Figure 2-8
The *Records* pull-down menu

The blank edit screen appears (Figure 2-7).

4. Enter the next five records for this file in the same way you entered the first five (refer to Figure 2-5). The last record should be Beverage Board.

5. Terminate by selecting *Exit/Exit*.

You are returned to the Control Center.

6. To see the full impact of the next sequence of steps, end this session of dBASE by selecting *Exit/Quit to DOS* from the Control Center.

Adding Records Through the Browse Screen

In this next sequence, you will enter the remainder of the records through another screen format called the browse screen.

1. Bring dBASE back up. From the Control Center move the highlight to CUSTOMER and press F2

2. If the edit screen is displayed, press F2

Your screen will look like Figure 2-9. (If you see only the last record, press Page Up.) This is called the **browse** screen. The COMPANY field of the first record (JP Designs, Inc.) is highlighted and the status bar displays *Rec 1/10*.

Figure 2-9

The browse screen

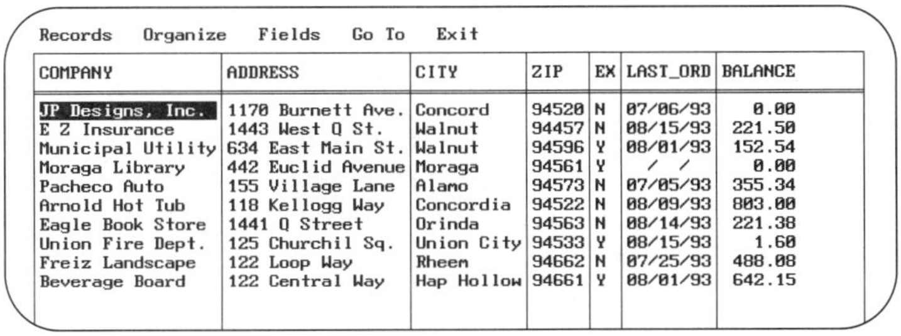

Records	Organize	Fields	Go To	Exit			
COMPANY	ADDRESS	CITY	ZIP	EX	LAST_ORD	BALANCE
JP Designs, Inc.	1170 Burnett Ave.	Concord	94528	N	07/06/93	0.00
E Z Insurance	1443 West Q St.	Walnut	94457	N	08/15/93	221.50
Municipal Utility	634 East Main St.	Walnut	94596	Y	08/01/93	152.54
Moraga Library	442 Euclid Avenue	Moraga	94561	Y	/ /	0.00
Pacheco Auto	155 Village Lane	Alano	94573	N	07/05/93	355.34
Arnold Hot Tub	118 Kellogg Way	Concordia	94522	N	08/09/93	883.00
Eagle Book Store	1441 Q Street	Orinda	94563	N	08/14/93	221.38
Union Fire Dept.	125 Churchill Sq.	Union City	94533	Y	08/15/93	1.60
Freiz Landscape	122 Loop Way	Rheen	94662	N	07/25/93	488.08
Beverage Board	122 Central Way	Hap Hollow	94661	Y	08/01/93	642.15

You can toggle between the browse and edit screens with F2 .

3. Press F2 , then press it again to return to the browse screen.

4. Records are appended through the browse screen in exactly the same way as with the edit screen; that is, select the menu option *Records/Add records*.

The highlight should now be positioned after the last line (record) in the browse screen.

5. You are now ready to enter the record for the Board of Ed. (number 11 of Figure 2-5). Enter the company name, address, and city exactly as you did from within the edit screen.

Note that the ZIP code for this record is the same as that for the preceding record (Beverage Board). dBASE conveniently allows you to copy the contents of a field from the preceding record into the corresponding field of the record being entered using the DITTO command.

6. Press Shift-F8

The value from the record 10 ZIP field is copied to the ZIP field of the new record.

7. Continue entering the data for record 11. After you enter the balance amount, the highlight moves to the next line, awaiting entry of the next record.

8. Enter the data for records 12 through 16.

After the last record is entered, the highlight moves to a blank line.

9. Terminate data entry with *Exit/Exit*.

You now have the full 16 records entered into your CUSTOMER file, so end this session of dBASE with *Exit/Quit to DOS*.

. . . .

CATALOGS IN DBASE

Changing the Catalog Name

Examples that you study in this book are relatively few in number. However, in a work environment you would likely deal with numerous applications. Over time, the number of data and other types of files grows significantly and, if some organization is not maintained, can lead to real confusion. To avoid this, one means that dBASE provides is the catalog facility. A catalog is simply a list of files for a given application. For instance, you might have a customer catalog, an employee catalog, and an inventory catalog. Any file on your disk can be listed in one or more catalogs. Needless to say, a file must exist on disk before its name can be listed in a catalog.

When you run dBASE for the first time from any disk subdirectory, dBASE creates two catalogs: CATALOG.CAT, which dBASE itself uses to list the names of the catalogs that have been created, and UNTITLED.CAT, which dBASE uses for files that aren't assigned to any other catalog. If you look at a directory of your subdirectory (or of your diskette if your files are on a floppy disk), you will see these two catalogs listed.

Since the catalog name UNTITLED.CAT is nonspecific, change it to CUSTOMER.CAT with the following steps.

1. Bring up dBASE. Press F10 from the Control Center to obtain the pull-down menu shown in Figure 2-10.

Figure 2-10
The *Catalog* pull-
down menu

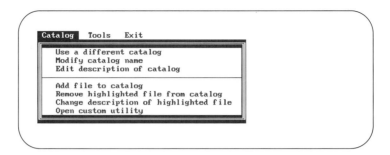

2. Select *Modify catalog name*.

   The menu will be overlaid with the following:

   Enter new name for the catalog: UNTITLED.CAT

   NOTE: Depending upon your disk configuration, subdirectory information may precede the display "UNTITLED.CAT".

3. Move the cursor to the letter "U" in "UNTITLED" and type **CUSTOMER**.

   It makes no difference if you use lower- or uppercase. Notice that the new letters replace the old ones.

4. Press ⌷Enter⌷

   You are returned to the Control Center.

   Your catalog is now named CUSTOMER.

Adding a File Description to the Catalog Entry

If there are many data files in a catalog, it is sometimes easy to confuse one with another if you have only the filename to look at. To overcome this problem, dBASE allows you to enter a description for each file displayed in the Control Center. To include a description for CUSTOMER, proceed as follows.

1. Move the highlight to CUSTOMER in the Data panel and access the *Catalog* menu (Figure 2-10).

2. Select *Change description of highlighted file*.

3. In the description box that pops up, type your description of this file. Typically, you could enter the following:

   Customer account balance file

When finished, press Enter

Now, both the name of the highlighted file and its description are displayed beneath the panels area of the Control Center.

OBTAINING PRINTED OUTPUT

As you will learn in subsequent lessons, dBASE has a wide variety of techniques for gaining access to stored data. For now, you can concentrate on a simple printed report.

From the Command Center, make certain the highlight is on CUSTOMER in the Data panel. At the bottom of the screen you will see *Quick Report: Shift-F9*. This is what you want.

1. Press Shift-F9 to access the pop-up menu shown in Figure 2-11.

Figure 2-11
The *Report* menu

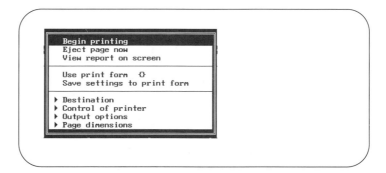

```
Begin printing
Eject page now
View report on screen

Use print form   ◇
Save settings to print form

▶ Destination
▶ Control of printer
▶ Output options
▶ Page dimensions
```

2. To see the report on-screen before printing it, select *View report on screen*.

    Follow the instructions at the bottom of the screen; you will eventually be returned to the Control Center.

3. To print your report, press Shift-F9 again. Select *Begin printing*.

    When printing is finished, you will be returned to the Control Center.

Your printed output should look like Figure 2-5. You will see that the column headings are the field names in the record. Also, a total for the BALANCE field is printed at the end of the report. The Quick report feature automatically totals each numeric field for all records in the report and prints the totals beneath the respective columns.

■ *SUMMARY OF COMMANDS*

Topic or Feature	Command Sequence or Key	Page
Add records to data file	*Records / Add records* (from browse / edit screens)	17
Browse to edit / Edit to browse	F2 (toggle between edit and browse screens)	18
Description for data file	*Catalog / Change description of highlighted file*	20
Display data	F2 (from Control Center)	15
DITTO: Repeat preceding field	Shift - F8	19
Exit data entry	*Exit / Exit*	17
Name catalog	*Catalog / Modify catalog name*	20
Print file structure	*Layout / Print database structure*	14
Quick report	Shift - F9	21
Save file structure	*Layout / Save this database file structure*	14

■ *REVIEW QUESTIONS*

1. What are the six data types in dBASE?

2. The following fields are to be included in a data file. Specify which data type should be used for each.

   Driver's license number

   Person's age

   Person's birthdate

   Automobile type

   ZIP code

   An indication of whether or not a person is a club member

   An indication of whether a person belongs to club A, B, or C

   Current mileage of a vehicle to be leased

3. Describe the factors that determine the width value for a field in defining a record.

4. What is the difference between creating a data file and entering records into the file?

5. How do you access a menu in dBASE?

6. Records can be entered into a file through either the _____ screen or the _____ screen.

7. What is the purpose of a file description in the catalog?

8. You have just brought up dBASE. What is the key sequence to begin adding records to the CUSTOMER file?

■ *HANDS-ON EXERCISES*

Exercise 2-1

Beginning in Lesson 4 you will be working with an invoice file. Create this file now for use in Lesson 4. The file, named INVOICE, must have the following structure.

Field Name	Type	Width	Decimals
INV_NUM	Character	4	
CUST_NUM	Character	4	
COLL_CODE	Character	1	
TRAN_DATE	Date	8	
AMOUNT	Numeric	6	2
PAID	Numeric	6	2
ENTERED_BY	Character	10	

After you have defined the file structure, enter the following records. Double-check your entries, as you will use this file for subsequent exercises.

INV_NUM	CUST_NUM	COLL_CODE	TRAN_DATE	AMOUNT	PAID	ENTERED_BY
2029	1441	C	07/22/93	677.84	677.84	Jack
2041	1401	D	07/30/93	316.54	316.54	Harmon
2018	1234	A	07/14/93	854.12	0.00	Jack
2001	1002	A	07/05/90	255.34	0.00	Jack
2019	1361	C	07/14/93	8.00	0.00	Harmon
2066	1007	D	08/09/90	125.45	0.00	Jean

INV_NUM	CUST_NUM	COLL_CODE	TRAN_DATE	AMOUNT	PAID	ENTERED_BY
2056	1386	A	08/05/93	611.25	428.32	Jean
2078	1269	B	08/13/93	125.51	0.00	Jean
2057	1393	D	08/05/93	158.80	158.80	Harmon
2021	1183	C	07/17/93	155.67	0.00	Jack
2079	1228	C	08/13/93	222.50	1.00	Harmon
2044	1441	D	08/01/93	452.54	300.00	Jean
2045	1401	D	08/01/93	346.85	346.85	Alice
2032	1393	B	07/24/93	122.40	122.40	Alice
2060	1007	C	08/06/90	436.51	200.00	Harmon
2010	1361	B	07/08/93	542.19	0.00	Jack
2086	1228	D	08/15/93	255.40	255.40	Alice
2035	1183	D	07/25/93	332.41	0.00	Alice
2005	1002	C	07/05/90	155.93	55.93	Jean
2087	1298	D	08/15/93	245.60	244.00	Jean
2088	1269	C	08/16/93	45.82	45.82	Alice
2061	1333	D	08/06/93	534.81	534.81	Jack
2083	1386	D	08/14/93	88.92	50.00	Harmon
2084	1228	C	08/14/93	332.58	332.58	Jean
2052	1234	C	08/04/93	225.89	0.00	Jack
2040	1401	C	07/30/93	642.15	0.00	Jean
2073	1269	A	08/11/93	125.45	0.00	Alice
2014	1361	B	07/11/93	96.36	0.00	Jack
2006	1211	B	07/06/93	225.88	225.88	Harmon
2002	1007	A	07/05/93	441.04	0.00	Harmon
2090	1401	D	04/11/93	500.00	475.00	Jean

Exercise 2-2   A group of bikers maintains a database file of their progress. Create a data file (named BIKERS) consisting of the following fields.

Field	Field Name	Type	Width
Last name	LAST	Character	10
First name	FIRST	Character	10
Birthdate	BIRTH	Date	8
Club name	CLUB	Character	12
Best placement	BEST	Numeric	2
Earned points	POINTS	Numeric	3

The first record in the file must be one for you. ENTER YOUR LAST NAME WITH A PLUS SIGN IN FRONT OF IT. For instance, *Fred Jones* would enter *+Jones* for a last name. Enter appropriate values for birthdate and other fields. Following are the other records to enter into this file. For all character fields, use upper- and lowercase as shown; *do not use all uppercase.*

Last Name	First Name	Birthdate	Club	Best Finish	Points
Kimball	Gale	04/13/70	Roadrunners	01	075
Baur	Kirstin	07/06/69	Felines	08	029
Fillmore	Nancy	11/05/72	Roadrunners	06	037
Murphy	Belynda	06/02/74	Quicksilver	02	055
Yancy	Gloria	03/30/72	Felines	08	023
Gordon	Aileen	10/17/74	Roadrunners	09	020
Alton	Joanne	04/11/75	Felines	07	036
Westfall	Florence	08/10/73	Roadrunners	04	044
Noyes	Diane	02/05/68	Quicksilver	02	056
Zucker	Ida	10/23/67	Felines	01	075
Murphy	Andrea	06/14/73	Quicksilver	02	055
Gloor	Judy	04/18/68	Roadrunners	07	036
O'Conner	Laura	12/05/67	Felines	01	084
Porter	Kyle	02/18/74	Felines	03	046
Eliot	Janet	04/09/76	Roadrunners	02	061

Turn in the following to your instructor:

1. A printout of the file structure.

2. A printout of the records in the file.

Changing Data in the Data Files

OBJECTIVES

In this lesson you will learn how to:

- Make a backup copy of a data file.
- Work with the catalog.
- Modify the structure of the data file (adding and deleting fields from the record definition).
- Move around in the file.
- Edit records through both the browse and edit screens.
- Use the variety of browse options.
- Remove records from a file.

■ ■ ■ ■ ■ ■ ■ ■ ■ ■
BACKUP OF FILES

Making Backup Copies of Files

In using a computer, it is important to protect against loss of data. For instance, what if you had just completed a database term project and accidentally deleted your main data file without realizing it? The insurance against such a possibility is to periodically make a copy of files you maintain. Such a "reserve" is commonly called a **backup** copy.

Making a backup of the CUSTOMER file is important because in this lesson you will be changing its structure. In the real-world environment, structures of data files are occasionally changed by adjusting the widths of fields and by adding or deleting fields. Making any structural changes to a data file without first making a backup copy is foolish; it is far too easy to make a mistake and lose data.

For the exercises that follow, you will make two copies of CUSTOMER: one called CUST_ORG (for CUSTomer ORiGinal) and the other named CUST_TMP (for CUSTomer TeMPorary). To make copies of data files through dBASE you must work through the Query panel, a subject not covered until

Lesson 6. So for the time being just carry out the following sequence of steps; do not worry about trying to understand the query screen for now.

1. Make CUSTOMER the active file (open it) by moving the highlight to it and pressing [Enter]

   The highlight in the pop-up screen will be on the *Use file* option. That is the one you want, so press [Enter] again. CUSTOMER is now listed above the line in the Data panel, telling you that it is the file currently in use (open).

2. From the Queries panel select *<create>*.

   A list of fields from CUSTOMER appears across the top and bottom of the screen.

3. From the menu select *Layout / Write view as database file*.

4. In response to the prompt *Enter filename*, type **CUST_ORG** and press [Enter]

5. In response to the prompt *Edit the description . . .* type:

   Customer account file (original form—no Customer Num) [Enter]

6. After the file is created, control is returned to the query design screen; repeat steps 3–5 using the following for filename and description.

   CUST_TMP

   Work copy of Customer account file

7. To terminate, press [Esc]. Confirm that you wish to abandon by typing **Y**

You now have three copies of the customer file: CUSTOMER, CUST_ORG, and CUST_TMP. They are listed in the Data panel together with any files you created in Lesson 2.

Exercises in this lesson involve both CUSTOMER and CUST_TMP; you will be switching back and forth between the two files. Before you begin each session, be certain to check the status bar to ensure you have the correct file.

. . . .

DELETING A FIELD FROM THE FILE STRUCTURE

Ultimately, you will change the file structure of CUSTOMER by adding one field and changing the name of another. First, however, use CUST_TMP to delete a field.

The Delete Sequence

For this first exercise, you will delete the LAST_ORD field of the CUST_TMP file, and then return to the Control Center. If you are not already in dBASE, bring it up.

1. From the Control Center highlight CUST_TMP in the Data panel.

2. Select the design mode with Shift-F2 (refer to the bottom of the screen: *Design:Shift-F2*). Alternately, you could press Enter and select the *Modify structure/order* menu option.

3. Press Esc to get rid of the menu. Your screen displays the file structure (refer to Figure 2.4).

4. Move the highlight down to the LAST_ORD field.

5. Check the information line at the bottom of the screen and you will see

    Insert/Delete field:Ctrl-N/Ctrl-U

    You want to delete this field, so use the Ctrl-U combination. The LAST_ORD field is removed and the BALANCE field is moved up to number 6.

6. Your task is completed, so you can return to the Control Center. Select *Exit/Save changes and exit*.

7. In response to the message *You have made changes . . .* type **Y** for Yes.

After deleting this field and rebuilding the file, dBASE will return to the Control Center. Before proceeding, check the file to be certain that dBASE did indeed remove the field. Press F2 (the Data key), and you are presented with the browse screen. If you have just completed the preceding sequence, only the last record in the file will show. Get to the top of the file with Page Up. Note that the last-order-date field is gone.

Whenever you modify a file structure by deleting or adding a field, dBASE creates a new file. It does this by copying, field by field, the records from the original file into a newly created file containing the modified structure. The new file is given the name of the original file and the original is deleted from disk. Thus, for a deletion operation, all data from a deleted field is lost. If you make an error and delete the wrong field, your only recourse (short of reentering the data) is your backup copy of the file.

MODIFYING THE STRUCTURE OF THE CUSTOMER FILE

Proceed now to the "real thing"—that is, modifying the structure of CUSTOMER. This exercise consists of two steps:

- Change the field name EX to EXEMPT.
- Add a customer-number field named CUST_NUM with the following characteristics: type—character, width—4.

On one hand, you can combine several field additions and deletions in a single structure-change sequence. On the other, you *cannot* combine changing a field name and adding (or deleting) a field in a single modifications operation because of the way in which dBASE copies the data from the original file to the new one. Thus the actions of this example must be done in this sequence: Change the field name and then save the structure; add the new field, then save the structure again.

Changing a Field Name

Begin by changing the field name.

1. From the Control Center, highlight CUSTOMER, then select design mode with (Shift)-(F2).

2. Press (Esc) to eliminate the pull-down menu.

   This produces the file structure screen of Figure 2.4.

3. Move the highlight to EX, line number 5, and make it EXEMPT.

4. Save this change through the *Layout/Save this database file structure* menu option.

5. You are prompted for the filename, with the current name CUSTOMER offered as a default. Press (Enter) to accept the default.

6. You receive the message:

   Should data be COPIED from backup for all fields?

   Note that this does not refer to the backup copy that you made but to the original CUSTOMER file from which you made the field name change. Respond by typing **Y** for Yes.

7. In response to the message *Should all data be copied . . .* type **Y** for Yes.

8. In response to the message *You have made changes . . .* type **Y** for Yes.

   The change (EX to EXEMPT) is made, and control is returned to the structure design screen.

9. To check your file, press (F2) then (Page Up) to display the entire file.

   Notice that the data is unchanged but the field name EX is now EXEMPT.

Adding the Customer-Number Field

With the field name change completed, you can now proceed to add a customer-number field to this data file structure.

1. From the browse screen, return to design mode with Shift-F2. Press Esc to remove the resulting menu.

2. Position the highlight on the first field, the place you wish to insert the customer-number field. Use Ctrl-N to open a new line. All fields will be moved down one line and the first line will be blank.

3. Make the following entries for this field:

Name:	CUST_NUM
Type:	Character
Width:	4

Your design screen should appear as shown in Figure 3-1.

Figure 3-1

The final structure of CUSTOMER

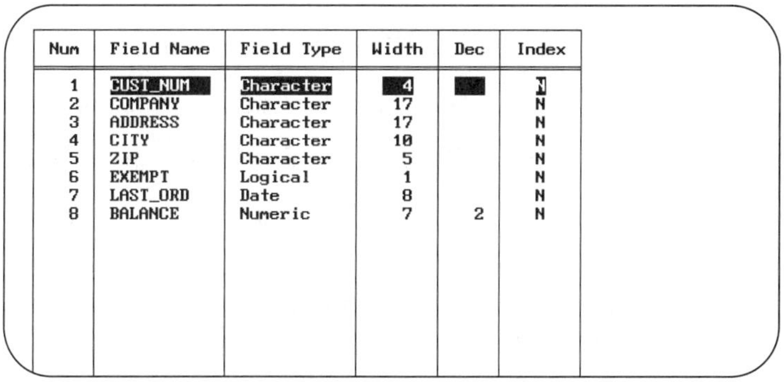

Num	Field Name	Field Type	Width	Dec	Index
1	CUST_NUM	Character	4		N
2	COMPANY	Character	17		N
3	ADDRESS	Character	17		N
4	CITY	Character	10		N
5	ZIP	Character	5		N
6	EXEMPT	Logical	1		N
7	LAST_ORD	Date	8		N
8	BALANCE	Numeric	7	2	N

4. To terminate, select *Exit / Save changes and exit.*

5. Confirming with the letter **Y** for Yes causes the new CUSTOMER file to be created with the customer-number field.

After a moment, the Control Center reappears.

Checking the New Version of CUSTOMER

Before winding up this session, check the file to see what you have accomplished. From the Control Center, press F2 to display the data and Page Up to view the entire file on-screen. There are two items you should notice.

First, the customer number is blank for every record (you created the field but you have not yet entered data into it). Second, the balance field is not displayed on-screen. Do not be concerned; the browse screen does not show this field simply because there is not enough room. However, you can bring it into view by moving across the screen. Successively press [Tab] until the cursor moves to LAST_ORD (alternately, you can use [F4]). Then press it once more, and the screen scrolls to the left. CUST_NUM will go off-screen and BALANCE will come into view. You can move left field by field with [Shift]-[Tab] (alternately, you can use [F3]).

. . . .

MOVING AROUND IN THE BROWSE SCREEN

Because CUSTOMER contains only 16 records, moving from one record to another in the file is relatively easy. For instance, from the browse screen, you can hold down [↓] and quickly go from the first to the last record of the file. If your file contained 1600 records, however, you would need more-efficient means to move up and down in the file. To this end, dBASE includes a number of commands to get you from one record to another. Examine the *Go To* menu shown in Figure 3-2, which features eight options. You will try the first four in this lesson and the last four in a later lesson. Notice that the number of the record currently selected is displayed. For instance, if you have not performed other operations, you are at record 1; *Rec 1/16* on the status bar indicates the current record number and the total number of records in the file.

Figure 3-2

The *Go To* menu

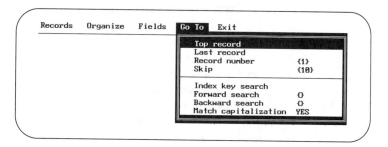

Experiment with some basics now. Access the browse screen for CUSTOMER (highlight CUSTOMER in the Data panel and press [F2]); clear the menu with [Esc].

1. Access the *Go To* menu.

2. Select the *Last record* option; notice that the highlight is now on record 16, the last record in the file, and the status bar displays *Rec 16/16*.

3. Select *Go To/Top record*; notice that the highlight is now on record 1, the first record in the file.

4. Select *Go To/Record number*; in response to the prompt, you will see a default value of 1. Delete this default, type **4**, and press [Enter]

Record 4 becomes the current record.

5. Select *Go To/Skip*; in response to the prompt you will see a default of 10. Delete it, type **9**, and press Enter. dBASE skips ahead nine records, and record 13 becomes the current one.

6. Try the skip again except enter –6. dBASE allows you to skip either forward or backward in a file.

As you can see, moving around in a file with these commands is relatively simple. You might want to try some options that are clearly not valid to see what happens. For instance, try to go to record 40 or skip 35 records in your 16-record file. Remember, the computer will not explode if you do something wrong.

· · · · · · · · · ·
EDITING DATA

For the next set of activities, use CUST_TMP so that you do not change the contents of CUSTOMER. Return to the Control Center, highlight CUST_TMP in the Data panel, and press F2 to get the browse screen. Before proceeding, check the status bar to be certain that CUST_TMP is the listed database file.

Overtyping and Inserting

Remember that when you are making changes to entries (editing), your keyboard can operate in either insert mode or overtype mode. In **insert** mode, characters are inserted at the cursor position, and other characters are moved to the right. Whenever dBASE is in insert mode, the abbreviation *Ins* is displayed on the lower right of the status bar.

In **overtype** mode the newly entered character replaces the character at the cursor position. The Insert key allows you to switch between these two modes. For instance, press Insert, and *Ins* appears in the status bar; press it again and *Ins* disappears. Press it a third time and *Ins* reappears. Keys that operate in this way are called **toggles,** because they toggle back and forth between two states. Experiment with one of the data fields in your browse screen.

Undoing a Change to a Record

Next, see what dBASE allows if you change your mind while editing a record.

1. Go to the first record in the file (JP Designs).

2. Change the name to CQ Designs and the address to **1234** (from 1170).

3. Without moving the cursor, lean back and take a look at your record. Oh no! You didn't mean to make that change!

4. Fortunately, to undo the change is easy. Bring up the *Records* menu (shown in Figure 3-3).

Figure 3-3
The *Records* menu

```
Records   Organize   Fields   Go To   Exit
   Undo change to record

   Add new records
   Mark record for deletion
   Blank record
   Record lock
   Follow record to new position
```

5. *Undo change to record* is highlighted, so press Enter

The menu disappears and the original values are restored to the record.

6. Repeat the preceding steps 1–5 except at step 3 move the cursor down to the next record.

In this last sequence, the changes you made remain; the original field contents are not restored. Sometimes the actions of dBASE (or any piece of software for that matter) can be most confusing if you don't know the rules of the game. In this case, when you are viewing records through browse, dBASE displays an entire screen full of records. However, dBASE is directly working with only the record that is highlighted, which is called the **current record**. Changes you make to the current record are held in memory. Thus if you want to undo the changes on-screen, dBASE simply substitutes the original field values from the record still stored on disk. Only when you move the cursor to another record (make another record the current record) does dBASE save the changes you have made.

You should be aware that all of these conventions for editing from the browse screen also apply to the edit screen. You could repeat the preceding sequence of steps using the edit screen.

BROWSE OPTIONS

Browse has some other options (not found in the edit screen) that make life easier when working with dBASE. They are available through the *Fields* menu (shown in Figure 3-4). Since you will be entering customer-number values using one of these options, open the CUSTOMER file. Remember, return to the Control Center, highlight CUSTOMER, and press F2 . Check the status bar to ensure that CUSTOMER is listed as the open file.

Figure 3-4

The *Fields* menu

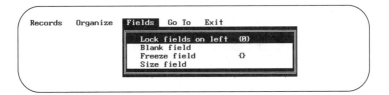

Locking Fields

1. From the browse screen of CUSTOMER select *Fields/Lock fields on left* (refer to Figure 3-4).

2. In response to the prompt

    Enter number of fields to remain stationary:

    type **2**. The menu disappears and the browse screen is unchanged.

3. By successively pressing Tab (or F4), move the highlight to the LAST_ORD field. Press Tab once more and BALANCE comes into view, ADDRESS disappears, and CUST_NUM and COMPANY remain.

The action of locking the two left fields causes scrolling to occur to the right of the two locked fields. This is especially convenient when you have a file with records consisting of many fields. For instance, assume that CUSTOMER contains several more fields each with numeric data. If you scrolled very far to the right you would not see the company name, so determining whose record you were looking at would be difficult. Locking fields avoids this problem.

Sizing Fields

Skip down to the last option, *Size field,* and see what choices dBASE gives you for changing the appearance of the browse screen.

1. Position the highlight in the COMPANY column (it does not matter on which record).

2. Access the *Fields* menu and select the *Size field* option. Notice the following below the status bar.

Change current column width: ↔   *End sizing:* ◄─┘

3. Press → several times and notice that the COMPANY column becomes wider. Press ← several times and the column becomes narrower. Continue until the COMPANY column is the same width as that in Figure 3-5.

Figure 3-5

Narrowing the
COMPANY column

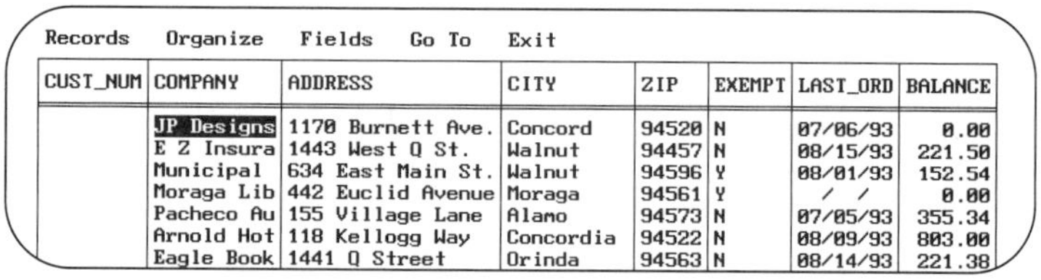

Records	Organize	Fields	Go To	Exit				
CUST_NUM	COMPANY	ADDRESS	CITY	ZIP	EXEMPT	LAST_ORD	BALANCE	
	JP Designs	1170 Burnett Ave.	Concord	94520	N	07/06/93	0.00	
	E Z Insura	1443 West Q St.	Walnut	94457	N	08/15/93	221.50	
	Municipal	634 East Main St.	Walnut	94596	Y	08/01/93	152.54	
	Moraga Lib	442 Euclid Avenue	Moraga	94561	Y	/ /	0.00	
	Pacheco Au	155 Village Lane	Alamo	94573	N	07/05/93	355.34	
	Arnold Hot	118 Kellogg Way	Concordia	94522	N	08/09/93	803.00	
	Eagle Book	1441 Q Street	Orinda	94563	N	08/14/93	221.38	

4. Press [Enter] to fix the column width.

5. Now try changing the EXEMPT column. From the browse screen, move the highlight to the EXEMPT column.

6. Access the *Fields* menu again and select the *Size field* option.

7. Press ← to narrow the column. dBASE beeps and will not narrow the column. You cannot make a column any narrower than the field name (serving as the column description) at the top. Press [Esc]

You should realize that any change you make to a column width applies to the browse display during that browse session. *It does not change the field width in the data file.* Furthermore, if you exit browse and then return, the columns are at their default settings.

Freezing a Column to Simplify Data Input and Editing

The next option is *Freeze field,* which provides a convenient means for entering data into the CUST_NUM field.

1. Access the *Fields* menu and select *Freeze field.*

2. In response to the prompt, type **CUST_NUM** and press [Enter]

3. Now try to move the highlight to other fields. Some of the keys simply do not work; others move the highlight up and down. In other words, activity is "frozen" to this column.

4. Position the highlight to the first record in the file.

5. Type **1211,** the customer number for JP Designs.

   Notice that when you enter the last digit into this four-position field, dBASE automatically jumps to the same field of the next record.

6. Enter the customer number for the rest of the records as follows.

Number	Company
1228	E Z Insurance
1441	Municipal Utility
1461	Moraga Library
1002	Pacheco Auto
1007	Arnold Hot Tub
1386	Eagle Book Store
1298	Union Fire Dept.
1183	Freiz Landscape
1401	Beverage Board
1269	Board of Ed.
1333	Baker Pool Serv.
1393	Coiffeur Hut
1361	CC Social Serv.
1199	Ramo's Tacos
1234	Carlson Metal

7. After you enter a value for the last record, dBASE gives you the option of entering more records with the following prompt.

   Add new records? (Y/N)

Respond with **N** for No.

To continue working on other activities, you could unfreeze this column by selecting *Fields/Freeze field* again. Then in response to the field name request, erase CUST_NUM (leaving it blank) and press Enter

The remaining option in the *Fields* menu is *Blank fields*. This does exactly as the name suggests; it deletes everything in the highlighted field (changes it to blank). If you want to try it, wait until you open CUST_TMP for the next exercise.

. . . .
DELETING RECORDS FROM A FILE

Marking for Deletion

In maintaining a database, not only will you need to add new records and edit existing ones, but you will also delete records you no longer need. This session shows you how to:

- mark records for deletion
- clear the deletion mark

Because you do not want to delete records from the CUSTOMER file, work with CUST_TMP once again. As before, check the status bar for CUST_TMP as the open file.

1. From the Control Center, highlight CUST_TMP and press [F2]

2. To delete the second record (E Z Insurance), move the highlight to it. From the *Records* menu select *Mark record for deletion* (see Figure 3-3).

Notice that the menu disappears but the record is still there. Temporarily switch to the edit screen with [F2] and you still see this record. Now look at the right side of the status bar. The word *Del* means that the current record has been *marked* for deletion but has not yet been removed from the file. dBASE allows you to make deleted records "invisible" so that they do not show during normal processing. The advantage of this feature is that you can clear the deletion mark from records, thereby restoring them for normal processing. To illustrate, clear E Z Insurance with the following steps:

1. Make certain the highlight is still on the E Z Insurance record.

2. Bring up the *Records* menu and compare it to Figure 3-3. Note that the third entry is now *Clear deletion mark* (since this record is already marked for deletion).

3. Select the *Clear deletion mark* option, and *Del* disappears from the status bar.

Perhaps you find the menu sequence a bit clumsy. Remember when you modified the structure, and [Ctrl]-[U] deleted a field entry from the structure? With the highlight still on E Z Insurance, try [Ctrl]-[U]. Notice that the record is marked for deletion. Press [Ctrl]-[U] again and *Del* is removed; the deletion mark is cleared from the record. As you can see, the keystroke combination is much quicker. Before ending this session, mark the records of both E Z Insurance and Arnold Hot Tub for deletion.

Removing Records from a File

At some point you might want to permanently remove the records marked for deletion. That simple matter, called **packing** the file, is a major reorganization of the file in which dBASE writes all the nondeleted records to a new file and deletes the original file. With the next sequence, you will pack CUST_TMP.

1. From the browse screen, bring up the *Organize* menu (shown in Figure 3-6). Before proceeding, notice that one of the options is *Unmark all records*. With this you can unmark all records in the file that have been marked for deletion.

Figure 3-6
The *Organize* menu

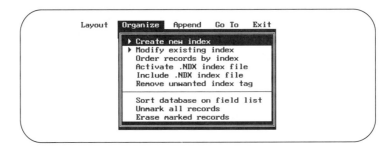

2. Select the *Erase marked records* option.

3. dBASE queries that you indeed want to do this. Respond with **Y** for Yes.

dBASE packs the file and when finished returns control to the browse screen. Inspect the file to see that the two records you marked for deletion (E Z and Arnold) are gone. (If either is still there, you did not have them marked for deletion.) Notice on the status bar that your file now contains only 14 records. Return now to the Control Center.

Deleting CUST_TMP from the Catalog

You are now finished with CUST_TMP, so you can remove its name from the catalog and even delete it from disk. If you want to experiment with it some more, you can re-create it after this exercise by following the backup procedure at the beginning of this chapter. For now, delete it. You should have the Control Center on-screen and CUST_TMP should still be the open file.

1. From the Control Center, Select *Catalog / Remove highlighted file* (refer to Figure 2-10).

2. Confirm that you want this file removed from the catalog by typing **Y** for Yes.

3. Because CUST_TMP is still active (open), you see the message:

   Cannot erase an open file

dBASE will not allow you to remove from the Catalog a currently open file. To close it, do the following.

   a. Press Enter to get back to the *Catalog* pull-down menu.

   b. Press Esc to get rid of the *Catalog* menu and return to the Control Center.

   c. Press Enter, then select the *Close file* option from the ensuing menu. The Control Center now displays the name CUST_TMP below the line, indicating that the file is no longer open.

   d. Make certain that CUST_TMP is highlighted then repeat the preceding steps 1 and 2.

4. You are now asked whether or not you want this file deleted from disk. Respond with **Y** for Yes.

Remember that the catalog is only a list of files you want to designate as part of a given application. Removing a name from a catalog list does not automatically cause the file to be removed from disk. In some cases you may want to remove a file name from a catalog but not delete the file from disk.

■ *SUMMARY OF COMMANDS*

Topic or Feature	Command Sequence or Key	Page
Access a record	Go To	31
Delete field	Ctrl-U	28
Design	Shift-F2	
Display next screen	Page Down	28
Display previous screen	Page Up	28
Freeze a field (browse)	Fields / Freeze field	35
Insert field	Ctrl-N	30
Lock field (browse)	Fields / Lock fields on left	34
Mark a record for deletion	Records / Mark record for deletion or Ctrl-U	37
Move cursor to beginning of record in browse or field in edit	Home	

Topic or Feature	Command Sequence or Key	Page
Move cursor to end of record in browse or field in edit	[End]	
Move cursor to first record	[Ctrl]-[Page Up] or *Go To/Top record*	
Move cursor to last record	[Ctrl]-[Page Down] or *Go To/Last record*	
Move cursor to next field	[F4] or [Tab]	31
Move cursor to previous field	[F3] or [Shift]-[Tab]	31
Pack a data file	*Organize/Erase marked records*	38
Remove a data file	*Catalog/Remove highlighted file*	38
Remove a deletion mark	*Records/Clear deletion mark* or [Ctrl]-[U]	37
Save file structure	*Layout/Save this database file structure*	29
Size browse column width	*Fields/Size field*	34
Toggle insert/overtype	[Insert]	32
Undo change to record	*Records/Undo change to record*	33

■ *REVIEW QUESTIONS*

1. What is the value of making a backup copy of a data file before you proceed to change its structure?

2. Explain the precaution you should take before changing the name of a field in a data file and adding another.

3. What is the difference between overtype and insert modes when editing?

4. What is the limitation on undoing a change you have made to a record from either the browse or edit screen?

5. Is it possible to change field widths of records from the browse screen by selecting the *Size field* option? Explain your answer.

6. What happens with the *Lock field* option of browse?

7. What happens with the *Freeze field* option of browse?

8. If a record is marked for deletion from a file, what takes place? Explain the rationale of this action.

9. How do you permanently erase records marked for deletion?

■ *HANDS-ON EXERCISES*

For this assignment you will be working with the BIKERS file created in Lesson 2, making changes that will form the basis for assignments in later lessons. You will also delete fields as well as records, actions that you do not want to do on your newly updated file. This means that you will need to make copies.

Exercise 3-1

Modify the structure by inserting the following fields:

NBA_NUM	Character	Width is 4	must be first field in record
STATUS	Character	Width is 1	must follow Club name
RACES	Numeric	Width is 2	must precede Best Placement

For STATUS enter a value of H (meaning Honorary) for the following three bikers: Fillmore, Gordon, and Gloor. For all others, enter a value of D (meaning Dues paying).

For NBA_NUM (National Bikers Association Number) and RACES enter the following data.

Name	Number	Races	Name	Number	Races
yourself	0772	?	Westfall	0989	6
Kimball	1150	6	Noyes	2212	4
Baur	2006	5	Zucker	1184	7
Fillmore	1609	6	Murphy	2896	5
Murphy	3910	4	Gloor	1918	7
Yancy	2829	6	O'Conner	2002	6
Gordon	1681	5	Porter	2771	4
Alton	2210	5	Eliot	2292	6

Print the file structure and a quick report. This will be your new file to carry over to Lesson 4.

Exercise 3-2

Working with a copy of your new file:

1. Modify the structure by deleting the BIRTH field and changing the field name BEST to BEST_PLACE.

2. Permanently erase all records with an H in the STATUS field.

Print the file structure and a quick report. After checking your work to make certain it is correct, you may delete this file from disk.

Creating and Using Forms

OBJECTIVES

In this lesson you will learn how to:

- Position fields that you wish to display.
- Include meaningful descriptions on the form.
- Display results of calculations using data from the record.
- Modify the way in which data from the record is displayed.
- Impose field-by-field restrictions on data that can be entered into a record.
- Use a form to view and edit data.

BASIC ELEMENTS OF FORM CREATION

The Value of Using Forms

As you learned in Lessons 2 and 3, you can inspect and enter records from both the edit and browse screens. Although you may have found these screens relatively simple to work with, they have a number of shortcomings. For instance, neither screen provides you much information regarding the data you are viewing. You know your field names because you created the file, but the average user of an application system will not have this familiarity. Thus a display screen that includes a descriptive title such as *Date of last order* will be much more meaningful to a user than one that displays the field name *LAST_ORD*. For this, you need more versatility than is provided by the standard edit and browse screens. This advantage is achieved in dBASE by **custom form screens**. A dBASE **form** is a screen through which you can both display and modify records in a data file. With forms you can:

- Include whatever descriptive information you feel is needed
- Select any fields from the data file that you require for the particular display
- Position the fields on the screen wherever you desire

- Include boxes, lines, and color for an easy-to-use presentation
- Create forms for displaying data which do not allow data entry
- Create separate forms for data entry and editing
- For forms that allow data entry and editing, control data values being entered

For your first form, you will create one to display data from the invoice data file you defined in the first assignment of Lesson 2. The end result will appear as shown in Figure 4-1. Notice that the form displays each field from INVOICE with ordinary English descriptions rather than field names. (In many applications, the screen form is designed to look as much like the corresponding paper form as is possible.) In addition to data from the record, the form can display calculated quantities as shown by the displayed balance (the difference between transaction amount and amount paid).

NOTE: If you did not create the INVOICE file in Lesson 2, do so now before proceeding.

Figure 4-1
A form for the
invoice record

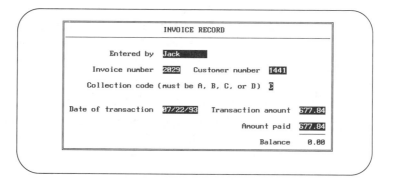

```
                        INVOICE RECORD

            Entered by  Jack

        Invoice number  2029    Customer number  1441

   Collection code (must be A, B, C, or D)  B

Date of transaction  07/22/93    Transaction amount  677.84

                                        Amount paid  677.84

                                            Balance    0.00
```

Entering Descriptive Information and Fields

First open the INVOICE file. Do so by moving the Data highlight to INVOICE and pressing [Enter] twice. Then proceed with the following.

1. From the Control Center Forms panel select *<create>*. Exit the resulting menu with [Esc], and the layout surface appears.

   The bottom two lines of the screen will look like Figure 4-2. Notice that the status bar indicates the location of the cursor (represented as a small block in the upper left of the layout surface). You can move the cursor over the surface with the arrow keys—try it to see what happens. Also notice the cursor. If it is a small square, you are in insert mode and *Ins* is displayed at the right in the status bar. If it is an underscore, you are in the overtype mode. Toggle [Insert] to see the change in the cursor.

Figure 4-2
Bottom of the form
design screen.

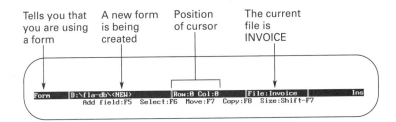

2. For the screen description INVOICE RECORD (see Figure 4-1), move the cursor to position 3,33 (row 3, column 33).

   NOTE: There is nothing magic about the screen locations used in this example. They were selected to give a nice-appearing, easy-to-read form.)

3. Type the description **INVOICE RECORD**

4. For the description of the first field to be displayed in the form, move the cursor to 6,21 and type **Entered by**

5. For data display from this field, move the cursor to 6,33. Use →, not Spacebar. To add the field to your display, press F5 (the *Add field* key as indicated below the status bar—see Figure 4-2). As an alternative, you can select the menu option *Fields/Add field*.

6. A pop-up menu appears, listing in alphabetic order all of the fields in INVOICE. Select the field ENTERED_BY.

   You will see a large pop-up menu that, among other things, describes the field you have just selected (you will explore some of these options later in this chapter). Instructions in the lower part of the screen say:

   When you have finished, press Ctrl-End to place the field on the work surface

7. Use Ctrl-End to complete this action.

   The upper portion of your screen should look like Figure 4-3. Notice that the data field area is highlighted and filled with the letter X. This is called the **field template** and is taken directly from the field definition of the record. As you will learn later, the X denotes a character position.

Figure 4-3
Partial form design

8. Proceed to the invoice number field. Move the cursor to the left across the ENTERED_BY display field—notice that it jumps across with one ← keystroke. This field is treated as a single entity. Move to position 8,17 and type **Invoice number**

9. Move to 8,33 with → and insert the field INV_NUM. Remember, do this with F5 , select the INV_NUM field, and end with Ctrl - End .

10. Enter each of the fields as you did the preceding two; screen locations are as follows.

8,40	**Customer number**
8,57	CUST_NUM
10,16	**Collection code (must be A, B, C, or D)**
10,57	COLL_CODE
13,12	**Date of transaction**
13,33	TRAN_DATE
13,44	**Transaction amount**
13,64	AMOUNT
15,51	**Amount paid**
15,64	PAID

When you designate the two fields AMOUNT and PAID, you will see that the fields are shown as 999.99. This is consistent with the three-digit decimal-point two-digit format defined in the record structure.

Saving a Form

At this point, you might feel like taking a break and reviewing what you have done. Even if you do not intend to take a break, it is a good idea to save your work periodically. You would not be very happy if you spent a few hours designing a form and then a power failure resulted in the loss of all your work. To save your work, do the following.

1. Select *Layout/Save this form.*

   If you wish to end this dBASE session, save your work and exit. This is done the same way as ending a file structure creation session. Select *Exit/Save changes and exit.* Alternately, you can use the Ctrl - End combination.

2. You are prompted with:

   Save as:

You can use any valid filename, but for this exercise type **INVOICE**

When you create a form, dBASE stores it to disk with the filename you designate and the extension SCR. For instance, your form is now on disk with the name INVOICE.SCR. dBASE also generates program code which actually does the work of accessing and displaying the data as defined by the form. There are two versions of the code, one with an extension of FMT and the other with an extension of FMO. Thus, when finished, you will see on your disk the three files INVOICE.SCR, INVOICE.FMT, and INVOICE.FMO. When modifying a form, dBASE always gives you access to the SCR file.

Entering Calculated Fields

If you are not still at the form design screen, return to it from the Control Center by highlighting INVOICE in the Forms panel and pressing [Shift]-[F2] (refer to the bottom of the screen).

For this form, one useful feature would be to show the balance owed on this invoice, which can be calculated by subtracting PAID from AMOUNT.

1. Move the cursor to 17,55 and enter the description **Balance**

2. Move the cursor to 17,64 with [→]. Press [F5] to access the *Fields* menu.

3. Select *<create>* in the *CALCULATED* column. In the resulting pop-up menu you will need to change two entries: *Expression* and *Template*.

4. To activate any line of this menu, position the highlight on that line and press [Enter]. Do this for the *Expression* entry and you will see {} replaced with the cursor. For this entry, you want a form similar to a mathematical expression to subtract PAID from AMOUNT:

    AMOUNT - PAID

    Assume that you cannot remember these field names. Look at the bottom of the screen and you will see

    Pick operators/fields: Shift-F1

5. Try it; press [Shift]-[F1]

    A pop-up menu appears, containing three columns; the left column is a list of field names.

6. Select the field AMOUNT.

    The pop-up menu disappears, and AMOUNT is included on the expression line.

7. Leave a blank space, type a minus sign, another blank, and then type **PAID**

NOTE: The blank spaces are not required, they simply provide easier reading.

8. Press [Enter]

   The expression is then enclosed within braces on the *Expression* line.

9. The default entry for *Template* was changed to 9999999.99 when you entered the expression. You want it to be 999.99. Move the highlight to that line and press [Enter]. Move the cursor left to the first 9 in the template, press [Delete] four times (giving 999.99), and press [Enter]

10. This completes definition of this calculated field. Press [Ctrl]-[End]

Your INVOICE form should look like Figure 4-4. To save your form before proceeding, select *Layout/Save this form*, or press [Ctrl]-[End]

Figure 4-4
The completed
INVOICE form

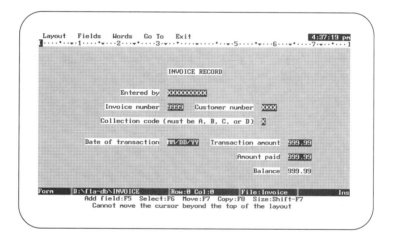

Adding Boxes and Lines

To complete this form, you only need to include the border (box) and separating lines (refer to Figure 4-1).

1. Move the cursor to screen position 2,10, the upper-left corner of the border around the display.

2. Select *Layout/Box*.

3. From the resulting pop-up menu, select *Double line*.

   A message appears at the bottom of the screen:

   Position upper left of box with cursor keys, complete with ENTER

4. The cursor is already positioned where you want the upper-left corner of the border, so press ⌷Enter⌷

A new message appears:

Stretch box with cursor keys, complete with ENTER

5. Move to 18,71 and observe the box as it "stretches." Press ⌷Enter⌷, and the box is fixed.

Now draw the line beneath the title INVOICE RECORD.

1. Move the cursor to screen position 4,11, the starting point of the line.

2. Select *Layout / Line*.

3. From the resulting pop-up menu, select *Single line*.

4. Because the cursor is already positioned at the starting point, press ⌷Enter⌷ in response to the prompt.

5. With ⌷→⌷ move to 4,70. Press ⌷Enter⌷, and the line is fixed.

Repeat steps 6–10 using screen positions 16,64 to 16,69 to draw a line beneath the Amount paid field.

Your form is now completed, so you can save it and exit.

Modifying a Form

Frequently after you have used a form for a while you will find that you want to change it. Changing a form is as simple as creating one. You can add or delete fields and text and you can move display items around. To illustrate, make some changes to the INVOICE form. Because this is only a practice exercise, do *not* save the modified form.

If you have gotten out of dBASE, bring up dBASE, highlight INVOICE in the Forms panel, and use ⌷Shift⌷-⌷F2⌷ to bring up the form design screen. Note the following on the bottom line of the screen.

Add Field: F5   Select: F6   Move: F7   Copy: F8   Size: Shift-F7

You have already used *Add Field* (⌷F5⌷) in creating your form. The *Select* (⌷F6⌷) command allows you to designate (select) a section of the screen. You can do the following with the selection.

- Move it to another place on-screen using the *Move* (⌷F7⌷) command.
- Copy it to another place on-screen using the *Copy* (⌷F8⌷) command.
- Remove it from the screen with ⌷Delete⌷

First, move the *Entered by* description and corresponding field to the right side of the form. As you perform each of these steps, watch the bottom line of the screen because it contains instructions for carrying out the commands.

1. Move the cursor to the letter *E* of *Entered* (position 6,21).

2. Begin the selection with F6 .

3. Move the cursor to the right edge of the ENTERED_BY field (position 6,42).

   The message on the next-to-last line of the screen says *Complete the selection with ENTER*.

4. Press Enter to complete the selection.

   The field is now selected and you can move it, copy it, or delete it.

5. Press F7 (*Move*) to indicate that you want to move the selected field.

6. With → move the field to the right.

   Notice that a "ghost image" moves but the field itself stays. Move it so that this portion of your screen appears as shown in Figure 4-5.

Figure 4-5
Moving a field on the form design screen.

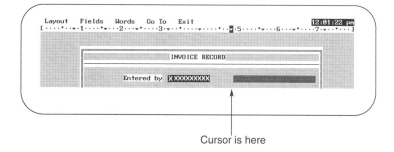

Cursor is here

7. Press Enter to complete the move operation.

   The field will jump to its new position. Use Esc to cancel the selection.

You may wish to experiment some more with changing the appearance of your form. Don't worry about really messing it up because you can abort the entire operation with Esc. Following are some tips to keep in mind.

- You can remove a selection at any time with Esc.
- If the position to which you move a description or field overlaps the original, you will be asked if you want to delete the covered text and fields. Answer Yes to this. However, abort the move if you are overlapping something else.
- Select a line in the same way you select a description.
- To select a box, position the cursor in the upper-left corner, press F6 , then Enter. You can then move the box in the same way you move text.

When you are finished experimenting, press Esc. Respond with **Y** for Yes that you do want to abort. You are returned to the Control Center, and your form remains unchanged.

. . . .
CONTROLLING DATA INPUT AND DISPLAY

Ensuring the Accuracy of Data

A critical issue in data processing is ensuring that data entry is error-free. Through user-defined forms, dBASE provides a variety of means for both controlling the input of data and displaying data in a more meaningful form. For instance, consider the customer number, which is defined as character. Even though customer numbers consist of only digits, you could enter letters or special characters through the edit or browse screens. On the other hand, by specifying an appropriate template in a form, you can limit data entry to only digits. As another example, consider the Amount paid field. You can enter any value from –99.99 to 999.99. However, you probably would not want a value less than zero or a value greater than the transaction amount. Through dBASE editing features, you can impose such control.

dBASE includes three capabilities that you can use to control the display of data in a file and the input of new data: field templates, picture functions, and edit options.

Controlling Input with Templates

You have already seen in creating the INVOICE form that dBASE automatically uses the X template symbol for character fields and the 9 symbol for numeric fields. The X designates that any character from the keyboard can be entered. The 9 designates (for numeric fields) that only digits, a sign, and a decimal point may be entered. Following are the symbols you will commonly encounter for character fields.

Symbol	Allows entry of
X	Any character
!	Any character but converts all letters to uppercase
A	Alphabetic characters only
9	Only digits 0–9

In addition to these, the characters #, N, Y, and L serve as template symbols. (When you select the *Template* option, dBASE displays a pop-up menu describing each of them.) If you use any character in a template other than these template symbols, that character will be inserted in the field as shown unless special action is taken to prevent it.

To experiment with template symbols, modify fields of the INVOICE form as follows.

Field	New template	Result
ENTERED_BY	!XXXXXXXXX	Will automatically make the first letter of the name uppercase
CUST_NUM	9999	Will allow entry only of digits for the customer number even though the field is defined as character
COLL_CODE	!	Will automatically make the code entered A, B, C, or D uppercase

Starting from the Command Center, highlight the INVOICE form and press Shift-F2 to access the form design screen.

1. Position the cursor on the screen template for the ENTERED_BY field and select the *Modify field* option from the *Fields* menu.

   This produces the pop-up menu shown in Figure 4-6.

Figure 4-6
The *Modify field* menu

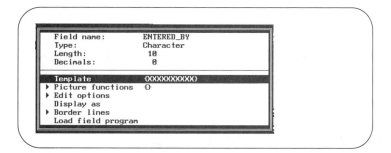

2. With *Template* highlighted, press Enter.

   The braces disappear and the cursor is positioned at the end of the current template XXXXXXXXX.

3. Move the cursor to the left and replace the first X with the character ! (exclamation mark); the template should now be !XXXXXXXXX. Press Enter to complete the operation.

   Once again, the template is enclosed within braces.

4. Use Ctrl-End to signify that you have completed this modification.

Repeat this process for the other two fields requiring template modification: change XXXX to 9999 for CUST_NUM, and X to ! for COLL_CODE.

These changes provide a small degree of control to data being entered into the three fields, however none of the changes causes the data file INVOICE to be modified. For instance, CUST_NUM still remains a character field; using the 9999 template in the form *does not change the field to numeric* in the data file. Controls of this form do not apply to the edit screen; if the form is not activated, the controls do not apply to the browse screen either.

Another useful template feature is the ability to insert punctuation characters. For instance, when you enter a date such as 12/18/83, the slashes can already be displayed on the screen, so you enter only the digits. What if you have a form in which you enter a Social Security number field that includes the hyphens, for instance, 123-45-6789. For this you could use the template 999-99-9999. Because the hyphen is not a template symbol, the hyphens would be included in the field automatically.

Other Control Capabilities

In the *Fields/Modify field* menu of Figure 4-6 there are two other options that allow you to control input. *Picture functions* includes a *Multiple choice* option that allows you to designate a list of the only allowable entries. Use this for the Collection code field and permit only entries of A, B, C, or D. When you receive the prompt *Enter multiple choices* type **A,B,C,D** (Enter).

The *Edit options* entry also provides several controls that would be useful to this form. For instance, you can designate the following: whether a field can be edited, a default value, a smallest allowable value, and a largest allowable value. Try some of these; they are reasonably easy to implement.

. . . .
ENTERING DATA THROUGH A FORM

After you save a form it becomes a cataloged element of your application. You can use it at any time to display and edit existing records in the file or to enter new records. Because the INVOICE file is empty, use the form to enter the thirty records listed in Figure 4-7. To do so, return to the Control Center; if you have terminated dBASE and are now restarting, move the highlight to INVOICE in the Forms panel.

1. Press (F2) for Data to retrieve your form; numeric fields contain zero and all others are empty (unless you designated a default value).

2. Proceed to enter data records in exactly the same way you did with the edit screen. When the cursor moves to the Collection code field, the first of the four options, A, will be displayed. To enter another value, press the letter or (Spacebar) to progress to the next allowable entry.

Figure 4-7

Data for the INVOICE file

```
Entered   Invoice  Customer  Coll.
by        number   number    code   Date       Amount  Paid

Jack      2029     1441      C      07/22/93   677.84  677.84
Julie     2041     1401      D      07/30/93   316.54  316.54
Jack      2018     1234      A      07/14/93   854.12    0.00
Harmon    2001     1002      A      07/05/90   255.34    0.00
Harmon    2019     1361      C      07/14/93    87.33    0.00
Harmon    2066     1007      D      08/09/90   125.45    0.00
Julie     2056     1386      A      08/05/93   611.25  428.32
Marion    2078     1269      B      08/13/93   125.51    0.00
Julie     2057     1393      D      08/05/93   158.80  158.80
Jack      2021     1183      C      07/17/93   155.67    0.00
Julie     2079     1228      C      08/13/93   222.50    1.00
Harmon    2044     1441      D      08/01/93   452.54  300.00
Jack      2045     1401      D      08/01/93   346.85  346.85
Julie     2032     1393      B      07/24/93   122.40  122.40
Marion    2060     1007      C      08/06/90   436.51  200.00
Julie     2010     1361      B      07/08/93   542.19    0.00
Julie     2086     1228      D      08/15/93   255.40  255.40
Marion    2035     1183      D      07/25/93   332.41    0.00
Jack      2005     1002      C      07/05/90   155.93   55.93
Julie     2087     1298      D      08/15/93   245.60  244.00
Harmon    2088     1269      C      08/16/93    45.82   45.82
Jack      2061     1333      D      08/06/93   534.81  534.81
Jack      2083     1386      D      08/14/93    88.92   50.00
Julie     2084     1228      C      08/14/93   332.58  332.58
Harmon    2052     1234      C      08/04/93   225.89    0.00
Julie     2040     1401      C      07/30/93   642.15    0.00
Julie     2073     1269      A      08/11/93   125.45    0.00
Marion    2014     1361      B      07/11/93    96.36    0.00
Harmon    2006     1211      B      07/06/93   225.88  225.88
Julie     2002     1007      A      07/05/93   441.04    0.00
```

3. As you enter the last field on the screen (Amount paid) the record is written to the file and the screen is cleared, awaiting entry of the next record.

4. After entering the last record, select *Exit/Exit*.

If at a later date you wish to add more records, do this with the following sequence (after highlighting the INVOICE form).

1. Press F2

This displays the first record in the file using the INVOICE form.

2. Select *Records/Add new records*.

In other words, after you select the desired form, the sequence is exactly the same as that for adding records through the browse or edit screens. After all, you are performing exactly the same function; you are simply using your own screen design rather than one furnished for you by dBASE (edit or browse). If you so desire, you can switch between your form and the browse screen by pressing F2 .

■ *SUMMARY OF COMMANDS*

Topic or Feature	Command Sequence or Key	Page
Add field to form	F5 or *Fields / Add field*	44
Change field	*Fields / Modify field*	51
Copy selection	F8	48
Insert box/line	*Layout / Box, Layout / Line*	47
Move selection	F7	49
Pick operators/fields	Shift - F1	46
Select screen section	F6	49
Save form	*Layout / Save this form*	45

■ *REVIEW QUESTIONS*

1. If you looked at your disk directory (from DOS) after saving the INVOICE form, you would see three different invoice files: INVOICE.SCR, INVOICE.FMO, and INVOICE.FMT. What are these?

2. What is meant by a *calculated field* on a form?

3. Is there a minimum or maximum number of fields that must be displayed from a record in designing a form? Explain your answer.

4. For what operations might you *select* a portion of the form design screen?

5. What is the sequence for selecting a section of the screen?

6. Someone tells you that you should not make the forms template for a field smaller than the field length in the data file or else the field length in the file will be changed. What is the fallacy in that?

7. Which symbol in a template causes character data to be entered in uppercase only? What character allows only digits to be entered?

8. You created the following template for an 11-position character field: **<!!!>99-XXX**. Give three different examples of data that might be entered into this field.

9. Why would the *Multiple choice* option not be used for a field such as the Amount paid (PAID)?

10. What is meant by *default value* for a field?

11. How would you create a form that allowed you to only view records from a file and not make any changes? Hint: Check the *Edit options* choice of the *Modify fields* menu.

■ *HANDS-ON EXERCISES*

Exercise 4-1

Create a data entry and display form for the CUSTOMER file that includes the following control on fields. *Note:* You will use this form in Lesson 5.

CUST_NUM, ZIP: Allow for entry of digits only

COMPANY, ADDRESS, CITY: Force the first letter to be uppercase

EXEMPT: Display No (N) as the default

LAST_ORD: Display the current date as the default

BALANCE: Do not allow negative values to be entered

Exercise 4-2

Create a data entry and display form for the BIKERS file that includes the following control on fields.

NBA_NUM: Digits only

LAST, FIRST, CLUB: Force the first letter to be uppercase

BEST, POINTS, RACES: Do not allow negative values to be entered

STATUS: Multiple choice options D and H with D the default

AVERAGE: Calculated value—points divided by races (POINTS/RACES)

FIVE

Indexing and Searching Data Files

OBJECTIVES

In this lesson you will learn how to:

- Designate that there be an index on a field through the file design screen.
- Create an index for a field or a combination of fields through the *Organize* menu.
- Select an index to control access to records of a file.
- Generate a report using an index to sequence records of the file.
- Directly access records of the file using an index.
- Directly access records of the file without using an index.

CONTROLLING ACCESS TO RECORDS

There are two ways in which records of the file can be processed: sequentially and directly. A particular application using CUSTOMER might involve printing a report with records listed in order by customer number. Records are accessed **sequentially** (one after the other) in customer-number order. Another application might require that a user update data stored in a specific CUSTOMER record. For this, the desired record is accessed **directly** by designating the customer number of the desired customer record. Then dBASE locates the exact record you want.

You had a brief introduction to direct access in Lesson 3. When using the browse screen, you accessed a selected record by using the *Record number* command and designating the record number. In actual applications, the physical number of the record usually has little meaning; a field that uniquely identifies each record such as the customer-number field is much more significant.

Principles of Indexing

The versatility of database processing revolves around the use of **indexes** to files. In everyday life using an index is nothing new. For example, the directory in a large building is an index. It displays a list of the building's occupants in alphabetic order, not in room-number order, and makes "direct access" of a particular occupant's room possible. For instance, to find the office of Dr. Hargrove, you would look up the name in the directory (index) and read the corresponding room number.

Similarly, an index to a file provides access to records in sequence based on a particular field or combination of fields. Using an index changes the **logical order** of the records in the file. That is, the **physical** or **natural order** is unchanged but the order in which records are accessed by dBASE is changed as dictated by the index. Indexes serve two useful functions for file processing. First, they are vital to directly accessing records and, second, they make it possible to process records in the file in an order other than their natural order.

Indexes in dBASE IV

Unlike previous versions of dBASE, dBASE IV includes special provisions for creation and maintenance of indexes via the Control Center. For each data file, a special index file is created. For example, corresponding to CUSTOMER.DBF is the index file CUSTOMER.MDX. Whenever you create an index through the Control Center, it is automatically stored as an independent index in the MDX file and is identified by a name, or **tag**, which you assign. The MDX file can contain up to 47 separate indexes (far more than you will need for exercises in this book).

CREATING AN INDEX

Designating an Index in the File Structure

In Lesson 2 you created the CUSTOMER data file. In doing so, for each field you designated its name, type, width, and for numeric fields the number of decimal positions. At that time, you ignored the *Index* entry (refer to the file design screen of Figure 2-2). For each field, this entry allows you to designate if an index is to be created and maintained.

For this exercise, you will return to the file design screen for CUSTOMER and designate indexes for two fields: customer number (CUST_NUM) and company name (COMPANY). By selecting the appropriate index, you will be able to view the file contents in either customer-number order or alphabetic order by company name.

    1. From the Control Center Data panel, highlight CUSTOMER. Enter design mode with [Shift]-[F2], then [Esc] to clear the menu.

2. From the file design screen with the highlight on the first field (CUST_NUM), tab to the *Index* column.

   The cursor will be under the *N*.

3. The message at the bottom of the screen tells you to change the option with the spacebar. Press Spacebar and the *N* entry changes to *Y* (for Yes).

4. Move the cursor to the second field (COMPANY) and repeat this process. When finished, the *Index* entries for both CUST_NUM and COMPANY will be *Y*.

5. Complete the operation with *Exit / Save changes and exit* or use Ctrl - End .

   dBASE proceeds to generate the indexes (tags). When finished, dBASE returns you to the Control Center.

Creating an Index Based on Multiple Fields

Processing needs commonly arise in which records of a file must be arranged in order within organized groups. For instance, a particular report might require that records of CUSTOMER be arranged in alphabetic order by city and within each city alphabetically by company name. For instance, customers in the city of Alamo would be listed in company order followed by customers in the city of Concord in company order, and so on.

 This application requires that the index operation be performed by concatenating (joining) the two fields CITY and COMPANY as follows.

CITY + COMPANY

To proceed with creating this index, make certain that CUSTOMER is highlighted in the Control Center Data panel, then enter design mode with Shift - F2 .

1. From the *Organize* menu select *Create new index* (shown in Figure 5-1).

Figure 5-1
The *Organize* menu

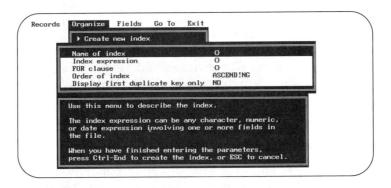

2. You first need a name for your index (index names have the same restriction as field names). With the highlight on the *Name of index* option, press (Enter), and the {} symbols are replaced with a flashing cursor.

3. For the index name type **CTY_COMP** (which indicates to you that it is a combination of the CITY and COMPANY fields).

4. Press (Enter) to complete the operation.

    The highlight progresses to the next menu entry, *Index expression*.

For the *Index expression* you must enter the expression on which you want the index based (CITY+COMPANY). As when creating calculated fields in form generation (Lesson 4) you can use (Shift)-(F1) to obtain the field list and other alternatives.

5. For this exercise, press (Enter), then type **CITY+COMPANY** and press (Enter)

As in Lesson 4, you can include spaces before and after the + sign if you feel it makes the expression easier to understand.

6. Complete the operation with (Ctrl)-(End) for return to the design screen.

7. Use *Exit/Save changes and exit* to return to the Control Center.

Indexing the INVOICE File

With the needed indexes created for CUSTOMER, you will now create indexes for fields of the INVOICE file: invoice number (INV_NUM) and customer number (CUST_NUM).

1. With INVOICE highlighted in the Data panel, enter design mode with (Shift)-(F2). Use (Esc) to eliminate the menu.

2. For the INV_NUM and CUST_NUM fields, change the *Index* entries of the file structure from *N* to *Y*.

3. Complete the operation with the menu selection *Exit/Save changes and exit* or use (Ctrl)-(End).

    You are returned to the Control Center.

There is one other index for INVOICE that will be necessary later for processing: the multiple-field index comprised of CUST_NUM and INV_NUM. This will result in invoices being grouped in ascending order of INV_NUM by customer number (that is, all the consecutive invoices for the first customer, followed by all the invoices for the second customer, and so on).

1. Access the design screen with Shift - F2 .

2. Select *Organize/Create new index.*

3. For *Name of index* enter: **CUST_INV**

4. For Index expression enter: **CUST_NUM+INV_NUM**

5. Complete the operation with Ctrl - End .

6. *Exit/Save changes and exit* returns you to the design screen.

. . . .
USING AN INDEX

Selecting an Index

When you first open a data file (or view one through a form), dBASE accesses records in the order in which they were written to the file. This is called a **physical** or **natural order** sequence. dBASE does not use an index automatically. However, after you open a file, you can select any index associated with that file.

1. With CUSTOMER highlighted, display it by pressing F2 . In the browse screen, note that records are displayed in their natural order.

2. From the *Organize* menu select *Order records by index.*

   As seen in Figure 5-2, a list of indexes (tags) for this file is displayed to the right of the *Organize* menu.

Figure 5-2
Index entries

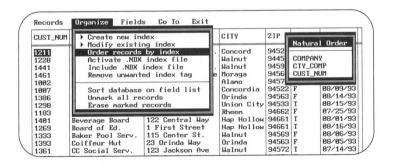

Move the highlight up and down and observe that the box to the left gives the field or expression on which the index is built. Notice that the index name is the same as the field name for indexes created by specifying an index in the file structure. The first entry (*Natural order*) allows you to deactivate the currently selected index and return to the physical (natural) order of the records.

3. Move the highlight to COMPANY (the company field index) and press [Enter] to select this index. Note that the records are indeed in alphabetic order by company name.

4. Access the menu again and select the CTY_COMP index.

In the resulting browse screen (Figure 5-3) look at the CITY column; the records are grouped alphabetically by this field (Alamo is first and Walnut is last). Next, look at the COMPANY column; within each city group, the records are in alphabetic order based on company name.

Figure 5-3

Records in company name sequence grouped by city

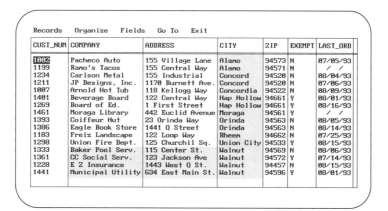

```
Records   Organize   Fields   Go To   Exit

CUST_NUM COMPANY           ADDRESS           CITY        ZIP     EXEMPT LAST_ORD
1002     Pacheco Auto      155 Village Lane  Alamo       94573 N        07/05/93
1199     Ramo's Tacos      155 Central Way   Alamo       94571 N          /  /
1234     Carlson Metal     155 Industrial    Concord     94528 N        08/04/93
1211     JP Designs, Inc.  1170 Burnett Ave. Concord     94528 N        07/06/93
1007     Arnold Hot Tub    118 Kellogg Way   Concordia   94522 N        08/09/93
1401     Beverage Board    122 Central Way   Hap Hollow  94661 Y        08/01/93
1269     Board of Ed.      1 First Street    Hap Hollow  94661 Y        08/16/93
1461     Moraga Library    442 Euclid Avenue Moraga      94561 Y          /  /
1393     Coiffeur Hut      23 Orinda Way     Orinda      94563 N        08/05/93
1306     Eagle Book Store  1441 Q Street     Orinda      94563 N        08/14/93
1183     Freiz Landscape   122 Loop Way      Rheen       94662 N        07/25/93
1298     Union Fire Dept.  125 Churchill Sq. Union City  94533 Y        08/15/93
1333     Baker Pool Serv.  115 Center St.    Walnut      94569 N        08/06/93
1361     CC Social Serv.   123 Jackson Ave   Walnut      94572 Y        07/14/93
1228     E 2 Insurance     1443 West Q St.   Walnut      94457 N        08/15/93
1441     Municipal Utility 634 East Main St. Walnut      94596 Y        08/01/93
```

Recall from the earlier discussion of indexes that creating or using an index changes only the logical order of the records (the order in which we see them). It does not change the physical order of the records in the file. With this in mind, make certain that the highlight is on the first displayed record (Pacheco Auto), and look at the status bar—this record is identified as record 5 of the file. Now move the highlight to the next record, Ramo's Tacos, and note that this record is still record 15.

Using an Index with Quick Report

Once an index has been selected for a file, that index remains active until you select another index, select the *Natural order* option from the *Organize* menu, or close the data file. One implication is that if you print a quick report, the records will be in sequence by the selected index. To illustrate, do a quick report for CUSTOMER using the COMPANY index as follows.

1. From the browse screen, activate the COMPANY index through the menu option *Organize/Order records by index*.

2. Use ⌗Shift⌗-⌗F9⌗ for a quick report.

3. In response to the pop-up menu, select *View report on screen*.

With the addition of the customer-number field, the line width of the report is greater than the width of the screen. As a result, each line of the report is displayed on two consecutive lines on the screen with the split in the middle of the date field. However, you can see that the records are indeed in sequence by the COMPANY field.

4. Follow the instructions at the bottom of the screen, and control is eventually returned to the browse screen.

5. If you would like a printed copy of the report use ⌗Shift⌗-⌗F9⌗ and select *Begin printing*.

6. When finished, return to the Control Center.

· · · · · · · · ·
DIRECTLY ACCESSING RECORDS IN A FILE

In Lesson 3 you directly accessed records of the file by designating the record number, an impractical method for most applications. More commonly, you will desire a record with a particular value in one of the fields. For instance, from CUSTOMER you might want the record for customer number 1002. Because the customer number is an indexed field, you could request dBASE to search the index and locate the desired record. On the other hand, if this were not an indexed field, you could request dBASE to search the entire file, record by record, until it found the record with 1002 in the customer-number field. Because the index is organized by customer number and is relatively small, an index search is much faster than a file search.

Refer to the *Go To* menu shown in Figure 5-4 (accessed from the browse screen). You are already familiar with the menu options above the separating line from Lesson 3. The *Index key search* option below the line is accessible only when you have activated an index. It is used exclusively for searching the index. The other three options pertain to searching the file itself without the use of an index.

Searching Using an Index

Rules for using an index key search on a character field are as follows.

Figure 5-4

The *Go To* menu

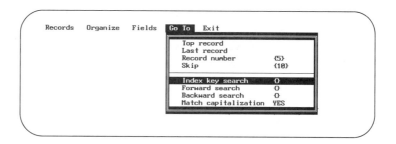

- The index key value (commonly called the **search string**) can be the entire field value or any portion starting with the first character of the field. For instance, if you were using the company name index in CUSTOMER and you wanted to find the record for Carlson Metal, you could enter as the search string:

Carlson Metal
Carlson
Carl

dBASE would find the desired record with any one of these because dBASE compares your search string character by character (from left to right) until it finds a match. Of course, only part of the field, such as *Carl*, might not give you the desired record, as it would also find such values as *Carl Funk* and *Carlo's*.

- As indicated earlier, the search is case sensitive. Thus if your search string is *carlson metal*, the record for *Carlson Metal* will not be found. (A solution to this problem is to use a dBASE function called UPPER in creating character indexes. Then always designate your search string in uppercase, for instance, *CARLSON METAL*.)

To give you some practice, try the index search using CUSTOMER and its associated index on the company name. Direct accessing of records can be done from the browse screen, the edit screen, or a custom form that you have created. In order to simulate how you would see direct access used in an interactive environment, use the CUSTOMER form you created in assignment 1 of Lesson 4. If you did not create this form, you can work from the edit screen.

1. If you will be working through your custom form of Lesson 4, carry out the following steps.

    a. Ensure that the CUSTOMER file is open in the Data panel.

    b. Move the highlight to the customer form in the Forms panel and press F2

2. If you will be working through the edit screen, carry out the following steps.

   a. With the highlight on CUSTOMER in the Data panel, press F2

   b. When the browse screen comes up, press F2 again to switch to the edit screen.

3. Activate the COMPANY index by selecting *Organize/Order records by index*.

   The displayed record should become that for Arnold Hot Tub (6/16), the first record in the company name sequence.

4. Access the *Go To* menu (Figure 5-2) and select *Index key search*.

   The following two-line prompt appears.

   Enter search string for

   COMPANY:

   Notice that the second line displays the index expression, COMPANY in this case, used in generating the index (this is simply a reminder to you).

5. Type **Carl** and press Enter

   The menu disappears and the record for Carlson Metal is displayed.

To give you an idea of how general the search can be, use a search string of the letter *C*. Then see how to progress from one qualifying record to the next.

6. Select *Go To/Index key search* and enter **C** as the search string.

   The screen displays the record for CC Social Serv., the first record with a name starting with the letter *C*.

7. Press Page Down, and the screen displays the next record (Carlson Metal); remember, *CC* comes before *Ca* because uppercase letters come before lowercase letters.

8. Press Page Down again and you will see the record for Coiffeur Hut.

9. To give you an idea of what happens if you make a mistake, try searching for *Ramo's Tacos*. Select *Go To/Index key search* and enter **Ramos** (omitting the apostrophe) as the search string. You will see the message *Not Found* indicating that there is no record with an index matching your search string.

To get an overall picture of what takes place while searching, switch to the browse screen (with F2) and repeat the preceding searches. Note that you need not repeat steps 7 and 8, as succeeding records are clearly visible on this screen.

. . . .
SEARCHING WITHOUT USING AN INDEX

The next search technique allows you to search a data file using any field in the record without the need for an index. Working with the small sample data files you have created, you will observe that records are accessed just as quickly without using an index as they are with one. However, access via an index is far faster than searching an entire file, and the difference would be quite noticeable with a large file. On the other hand, there are situations where the relative inflexibility of an index search simply does not satisfy your searching needs.

Basic Searching

Assume that you want to look at the record of one of the customers in the city of Walnut. If you are continuing from the preceding sequence, deactivate the index by bringing up the *Organize/Order records by index* menu and selecting *Natural order*. If you are beginning a new dBASE session, open the CUSTOMER data file and bring up your customer form on the edit screen.

1. You will be searching on the CITY field, so position the cursor to the CITY field on the screen. This is the way in which you identify for dBASE the field on which you wish to perform the search.

2. Access the *Go To* menu (Figure 5-4).

   Notice the *Match capitalization* option which displays *YES* as the default. (If you toggle this to *NO* by pressing (Enter), the search will be performed without regard to upper/lowercase.)

3. Select *Forward search*.

4. In response to the search string request, type **Walnut** and press (Enter).

   The record for E Z Insurance (record 2) should be displayed; this is the first record in the file with Walnut for the city entry.

5. To look at the next record with Walnut for city use (Shift)-(F4).

   This should give you Municipal Utility (record 3). Repeat this and you will see record 12, then record 14, and then record 2 again. After the last record meeting the search condition, access repeats from the beginning of the file.

As you can see, the *Forward search* starts with the current record and proceeds to the next record, then the next, and so on until a match is found. The *Backward search* option is identical except that the search progresses backward through the file.

Wildcard Searches

Database systems provide broad capabilities for searching on a portion of a field. Consider the following typical examples.

- Search for a record with a last-order date in the month of July
- Search for a customer located somewhere on the street Euclid
- Search for a record with 946 as the first three digits of the ZIP code (you have already done this type of search through an index)

In each of these cases you want to search on part of a field. For this application, dBASE provides the **wildcard characters ?** and *. Try them with the CUSTOMER file from your custom form screen or from the edit screen as follows .

1. Select *Go To/Top record*. (This may not be necessary but it will get you started from a known position in the file if you are continuing from the preceding exercise.)

2. Position the cursor on the LAST_ORD field.

3. Select *Go To/Forward search*; for the search string, enter **07/??/93**.

4. The first record found is that for Pacheco Auto, the fifth record in the file. Press [Shift]-[F4] repeatedly to see succeeding records. There should be four in this file, unless you have added or deleted records.

As you can see from this example, each ? wildcard character effectively says: "anything can occupy this single position." Note that 07/?/93 or 07/???/93 would not work; the count of ? characters must correspond to the number of "free" positions in the search.

The second example is considerably more complicated: the search must be for the word *Euclid* anywhere in the ADDRESS field. In this case, you do not know how many characters precede the search string or how many follow it. dBASE provides for this need with the * wildcard character, which says that any number of characters can be present.

1. Position the cursor on the ADDRESS field (still the CUSTOMER file).

2. From the menu select *Go To/Forward search*.

3. Enter as the search string ***Euclid***

4. The record for Moraga Library will be displayed.

Here the * wildcard character says "any collection of characters (or none at all)." This search string tells dBASE to look for Euclid anywhere in the address field. The following entries in this field would all result in successful searches: *442 Euclid, Euclid #14, 122 Euclid Way*, and *Euclid* by itself.

For the third example, searching for a record with a ZIP code starting with 946, you can use a search string of either *946??* or *946** since all ZIP code entries contain exactly five digits. On the other hand, consider an application in which the ZIP code field width were 10 and some records contained the four-digit extension (for example, 94663-1867) and others contained only the first five digits. Then the simplest form to use would be *946**. You could use 946???????, but there is no reason to do so.

■ SUMMARY OF COMMANDS

Topic or Feature	*Command Sequence or Key*	*Page*
Change order of records	*Organize/Order records by index*	60
Create an index	*Organize/Create new index*	58
Find next record	Shift - F4	65
Index search	*Go To/Index key search*	64
Search for a record	*Go To/Forward search* or *Backward search*	65

■ REVIEW QUESTIONS

1. The order in which records were entered into the file is called the _____ order or the _____ order. The order of records when viewed through an index is called a _____ order.

2. In dBASE IV, indexes (also called tags) are stored in a file with an extension of _____.

3. What is meant by the term *case sensitive*?

4. What special consideration would be necessary in creating an index for INVOICE on a combination of the customer-number fields and the amount field? Note: This question will require some imagination on your part; the topic is not covered in the lesson.

5. What is the maximum number of indexes that you can store in a single .MDX index file?

6. Assume that you want to do an index search and that the highlight in the *Go To* menu cannot be positioned at the *Index key search* option. What is wrong?

7. What is the advantage of using an index search instead of a non-indexed record search?

8. What is the advantage of the non-indexed record search over the index search?

9. How are the ? and * wildcard characters used?

■ *HANDS-ON EXERCISE*

Exercise 5-1   For the BIKERS file create indexes for the following:

NBA number

Last name and first name

Club name and NBA number

Print a quick report based on each of these three indexes.

Designing and Using Queries

OBJECTIVES

In this lesson you will learn how to:

- Define a wide variety of conditions to control records displayed.
- Use a query to inspect records in one or more files and to prepare quick reports.
- Change the sequence of records as viewed through a query.
- Select individual fields from one or more data files to be included in a query.
- Combine data from two files in a query.

INTRODUCING QUERIES

Forms of Lesson 4 provide you a means for controlling data entry and, to a limited extent, for controlling display access to data in a file. dBASE IV has a much more general feature for controlling access to data and for defining "views" of your data with which you can do the following.

- Control access to only those records of a file meeting your stipulated conditions. For instance, you might define a view of the CUSTOMER file that displays only those records with a zero value in the BALANCE field. In dBASE programming, this is called *filtering* the records so that only those meeting stated criteria are available.
- Provide access to all or part of the data in one or more files. You can use the view just as you would a data file to display the data and to produce reports. With some views you can even enter and edit data.

The second panel of the Control Center screen is the Queries panel. It is through this panel that you define and access your query files.

Creating a Simple Query

Before you begin, examine the **query design screen** shown in Figure 6-1. This screen is somewhat analogous to the form design screen in that it is the screen from which you define your query. Like the form design screen, it includes a menu bar at the top and a status bar and navigation line at the bottom. Unique to the query design screen are a **file skeleton** and a **view skeleton**. The file skeleton at the top includes the file name and, in successive boxes, names of fields in the file. The view skeleton includes similar boxes containing the names of the fields (and the file from which selected) that make up the view. Note in the file skeleton that fields of the file included in the view are identified with a down arrow in front of the field name. This particular view includes every field of the file.

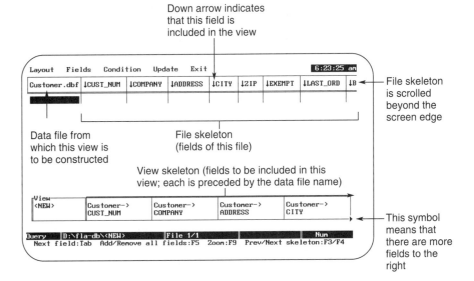

Figure 6-1
The query design screen

For your first query exercise, you will create one that displays only those records from CUSTOMER that have a zero balance (the BALANCE field contains 0).

1. From the Data panel open the CUSTOMER file.

2. From the Queries panel select *<create>*, and the queries design screen will appear (Figure 6-1).

3. To move the highlight from field to field use [Tab] (left to right) and [Shift]-[Tab] (right to left). Repeatedly press [Tab] and observe as the highlight moves. Continue scrolling to the right with [Tab] until you get to the last field in the record (BALANCE). If you press [Tab] one more time, the screen will wrap back to the beginning.

4. Use [Tab] to get back to the BALANCE field. You want all records from CUSTOMER with a BALANCE value of zero, so type the digit **0**.

5. To inspect your data through this view, press [F2]. (Note that this is the same key you use to inspect data in a file.)

The query design screen is replaced with the browse screen, displaying five records. (If you have the edit screen, press [F2] again.)

6. Tab across to the BALANCE field, which is currently scrolled off to the right.

   You can see that each of these records has a zero balance.

7. Return to the query design screen with Shift-F2.

8. You do not want to save this query, so press Esc. In response to the query regarding abandoning, press **Y** for Yes.

   You are returned to the Control Center.

Creating and Saving a Query

Now that you have had your first look at a query, you will take the next step and define one. Then you will save it so you can use it anytime you wish. This query will provide the following view of CUSTOMER

- The fields CUST_NUM, COMPANY, ADDRESS, CITY, and ZIP; in other words, omit the fields EXEMPT, LAST_ORD, and BALANCE.
- Only those records with a zero balance.
- Records in alphabetic order on COMPANY.

The first steps of this sequence are much the same as those of the preceding exercise. From the Control Center, make certain that the CUSTOMER data file is open then proceed as follows.

1. Select *<create>* from the Queries panel to obtain the queries design screen (Figure 6-1).

2. If the highlight is not beneath the box containing the filename (Customer.dbf), move it there. Use F5 (the Fields key) to remove all fields from the view.

   NOTE: If you press F5 again, the fields will reappear—this is a toggle key.

3. Move the highlight to the CUST_NUM field (actually, the highlight will be *beneath* the field). Watch the screen carefully and press F5 —a box "jumps" from the file skeleton to the the view skeleton. This depicts CUST_NUM being inserted into the view. Notice also that a down arrow has been inserted in front of the file skeleton field name. This tells you that the field is included in the view.

4. Insert the remaining required fields (COMPANY, ADDRESS, CITY, and ZIP) into the view in the same way as CUST_NUM.

5. Move the highlight to beneath the BALANCE field and type the digit **0**.

6. To tell dBASE you want the records in alphabetic order on COMPANY, move the highlight to beneath COMPANY.

7. Access the *Fields* menu (Figure 6-2).

Figure 6-2
The *Fields* menu

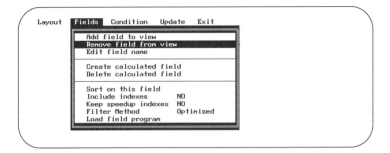

8. Select the *Sort on this field* option; a pop-up menu with four options appears. The first one, *Ascending ASCII*, is highlighted; select it by pressing [Enter]

Control is returned to the query design screen. Beneath the COMPANY box is the code word *Asc1*; this is one of many operands that can be used to control the view. Your design screen should be as shown in Figure 6-3.

Figure 6-3
A sample query design screen

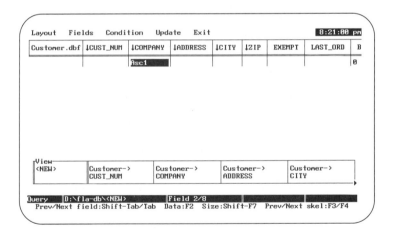

9. Design of your view is completed, so press [F2] to inspect your data; the browse screen should include five records in alphabetic sequence on the COMPANY field.

10. Use [Shift]-[F2] to return to the query design screen. The query is completed, so you can save it and return to the Control Center. Either select *Save changes and exit* from the *Exit* menu, or use [Ctrl]-[End]

11. In response to the prompt *Save as* type **ZB_CUST** (for Zero Balance CUSTomers) and press [Enter]

The screen message *Query saved to disk* appears, and you are returned to the Control Center.

In the Queries panel the name of your newly created query ZB_CUST is displayed above the line (meaning that it is currently open). Beneath this is the identifying line

File: ZB_CUST.QBE

The extension QBE indicates that this file is a set of program instructions describing to dBASE how to extract data from the CUSTOMER file according to your query specifications. It is not a data file.

Working with a Query-Created View

Creation of your query is now complete; the query is stored as part of your customer system. To illustrate that you can indeed use the query as you would a data file, try the following.

1. Close the query as you would a data file. (ZB_CUST will now be below the line in the Queries panel, indicating that it is no longer open.)

2. Move the highlight to ZB_CUST. Press F2 to display the data through the browse screen.

3. Exit browse either with Esc or through the menu.

4. Use Shift - F9 to print a quick report, and you will have a hard copy of your view.

5. You are finished with ZB_CUST, so close it.

SPECIFYING CONDITIONS FOR RECORD SELECTION

Designating Different Data Types

In the preceding example you used a filter on a numeric field (value of 0 for BALANCE) to limit the records in the view. As you probably expect, you can filter on any of the four data types you have used. However, queries require that you explicitly designate the type of data you are using (with the exception of numeric data). This is done with **delimiters,** which indicate the beginning and ending of data of interest. dBASE uses delimiters to designate data types as follows.

Data Type	Delimiter	Example
Character	" "	"Concord"
Date	{ }	{11/17/95}
Logical	. .	.Y. or .N.
Numeric	none	0

Querying on Character, Logical, and Date Fields

Try querying with each of these three data types using CUSTOMER. For the first exercise, assume that you want only those records with Concord entered in the CITY field.

1. From the Data panel open CUSTOMER.

2. Select *<create>* from the Query panel, which accesses the query design screen.

3. Move the highlight to the CITY field and type **"Concord"** as the filter condition.

4. Press [F2] to observe your view.

   The only records displayed should be those with Concord as the CITY entry.

5. Return to the query design screen with [Shift]-[F2].

6. Delete "Concord" from beneath CITY using either [Delete] or [Backspace] repeatedly.

Querying on logical fields is done in exactly the same way as with character fields. If you wanted to display all records that have an exempt status of Yes, the procedure would be the same as the preceding. Move the highlight to the EXEMPT field, type **.Y.** (do not forget the periods), then inspect your records from the browse screen. Return to the design screen and erase **.Y.**

Next try a condition on the LAST_ORD date field. You should have two entries with a date of 8/1/93. To confirm, enter **{8/1/93}** as the condition on the LAST_ORD field. (Notice that you do not need to enter the date as {08/01/93}; the leading zeros are not required.) Switch to the browse screen to inspect your display then return to the query design screen and erase the date.

Using Relational Operators in Queries

Each of the filter conditions you have tried thus far is based on the "equal" condition. For instance, in the first example your ZB_CUST view selects only those records with a BALANCE entry equal to zero; the character field example includes only records with a CITY entry equal to Concord. What if you want customers with a balance greater than zero or those not in Concord? For this, dBASE includes the following relational operators.

Operator	Meaning
=	Equal to
<> or #	Not equal to
>	Greater than
>= or =>	Greater than or equal to
<	Less than
<= or =<	Less than or equal to
$	Contains
Like	Pattern match (with wildcard characters)
Sounds like	Soundex match

If you terminated after the previous exercise, then bring dBASE back up, open CUSTOMER, and select *<create>* from the Query panel. If you are continuing, make certain there are no query entries in any of the fields.

1. To create a query that produces all records with a value for BALANCE greater than zero, enter **>0** for the condition under BALANCE.

2. Check your display from the browse screen then return to the query design screen.

3. Delete the query condition for BALANCE.

4. To create a query that produces all records for which the last-order date is 8/1/93 or later, enter **>={8/1/93}** under LAST_ORD.

5. Switch to the browse screen and check your display; when finished return the query design screen and delete the LAST_ORD condition.

COMPOUND CONDITIONS

AND Conditions

Frequently you will need to create views involving more than a single test as the selection criteria. For instance, you might want to show all records for exempt companies in the city of Walnut. For this the filter condition would be EXEMPT is Yes *AND* CITY is Walnut.

If you place two or more conditions on the same line below the file skeleton, all of them must be satisfied for a record to be included in the view. Thus to obtain the exempt companies in Walnut (an AND condition), you would make the query entries shown in Figure 6-4. Make certain you have no other query conditions, then make these entries. Use $\boxed{F2}$ to inspect the view data; two records are displayed.

Figure 6-4
AND condition on
two fields

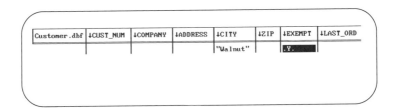

Sometimes you need to designate a range where you need both components of the AND on the same field. For instance, assume that you want a view that includes only those records with a last-order date between 7/20/93 and 8/10/93, inclusive. For this, you must require that the date be equal to or greater than 7/20/93 AND equal to or less than 8/10/93. In the query condition of Figure 6-5, you can see that the entries are separated by a comma.

Figure 6-5
AND condition on
a single field

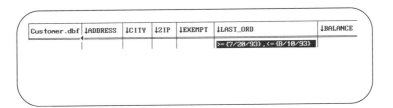

OR Conditions

Another application might require that your view include all companies that are exempt as well as those with a balance greater than zero. Here the filter condition would be EXEMPT is Yes *OR* BALANCE greater than 0. OR conditions are designated by inserting them on different lines below the file skeleton.

To try this, delete all conditions from the previous example. Then enter **.Y.** under EXEMPT. Next move to BALANCE, press $\boxed{\downarrow}$ to move to the next line, and type **0**. Your query should be as shown in Figure 6-6. Bring up the browse screen and inspect the records listed; those with .N. under EXEMPT all have balances of zero.

Figure 6-6
OR condition on
two fields

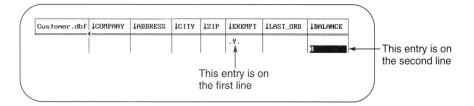

Figure 6-7
OR condition on
a single field

You can also have multiple OR conditions on the same field. For instance, if you wanted records of companies in the cities of Walnut, Orinda, and Moraga you would enter **"Walnut"**, **"Orinda"**, and **"Moraga"** on separate lines under the CITY field (Figure 6-7).

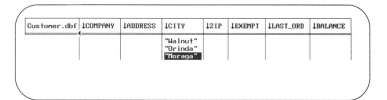

· · · · · · · · ·
ALTERING THE ORDER OF RECORDS

ASCII and Dictionary Sequencing

In the ZB_CUST view you designated that the records be in sequence based on the company name field. If you recall, in steps 6–8 of the exercise in which you created the view, you designated that records be sorted on the company name field. When you selected the *Sort on this field* option, the pop-up menu shown in Figure 6-8 was displayed. This list of four options represents the four ways in which a character field can be used to determine the order of records in a view. Of course, an ascending sequence is one in which the progression is from smallest to largest; a descending sequence progresses from largest to smallest.

Figure 6-8
Sort sequence
options

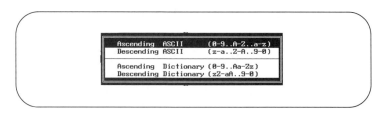

An ASCII sequence is one in which characters are ordered according to their ASCII values: uppercase letters before lowercase letters. Digits are ordered before any of the letters. On the other hand, a **dictionary** sequence produces a conventional alphabetic order that you would expect: lowercase letters and uppercase letters are treated alike.

Ordering by Multiple Fields

Just as you can create an index on two or more fields, you can designate ordering on multiple fields for a view. Assume that you want a view that lists records in order by city and within each city by date of last order. CITY will be the primary sorting field and COMPANY the secondary sorting field. (Although you created an index on this combination in Lesson 5, you will not use it for the next exercise.)

Before starting, return to the Control Center with Esc, then bring up a new query design screen for the CUSTOMER file.

1. Position the highlight beneath CITY in the file skeleton.

2. To designate the sort order, select the menu option *Fields / Sort on this field / Ascending ASCII*.

   When finished, *Asc1* will be displayed beneath CITY.

3. Move to the COMPANY field and repeat the process.

   When finished, *Asc2* will be displayed beneath COMPANY.

4. This designates sequencing on both fields: CITY then COMPANY. Press F2 to view the data.

You can see that the records are in the desired sequence. Notice also that this view is designated as *ReadOnly* in the status bar, meaning that you cannot edit or write new records to it. This is because dBASE has created a new temporary file and sorted it for this view. When you terminate the session, the temporary file will be deleted.

Accessing All Indexes

Through the *Fields* menu dBASE provides you full access to all indexes associated with a file. In fact, the previous example could have used the index on CITY+COMPANY that you created in Lesson 5. Let's find out how.

1. Return to the query design screen from the preceding exercise and delete the sorting entries from CITY and COMPANY.

2. Bring up the *Fields* menu and notice the *Include indexes* option; it is defaulted to NO.

3. Move the highlight to this option and press Enter

The menu disappears and control is returned to the design screen. Now both the CUST_NUM and COMPANY names in the file skeleton are preceded by a solid triangle (in dBASE IV Version 1.0, it is the # symbol). This indicates that the field has an index tag associated with it.

4. Move the highlight to the right until you come to the field designated CITY+COMPANY. This is called a *pseudo-field* and is displayed only because it represents an index.

5. With the highlight under this pseudo-field, select the menu option *Fields/Sort on this field/Ascending ASCII*.

When finished, *Asc3* will be displayed beneath the field.

NOTE: If you returned to the Control Center prior to beginning this exercise, ASC1 will be displayed.

6. Switch to the browse screen with F2; the records are in the proper sequence and the status bar does not include *ReadOnly*.

You are looking at the original data file through the index.

You can terminate this session with Esc. Respond appropriately to avoid saving the results of your experimentation.

MODIFYING THE VIEW

Calculated Fields

Assume that you would like this view to include a carrying-charge field which is calculated as 0.085 times BALANCE. The following exercise illustrates how to include calculated fields.

1. From the Control Center make certain CUSTOMER is still open, and select *<create>* from the Queries panel.

2. Remove all fields from the view (F5 with the highlight beneath Customer.dbf).

3. Insert CUST_NUM, COMPANY, and BALANCE into the view.

4. From the *Fields* menu select *Create calculated field*.

Another skeleton labeled *Calc'd Flds* is inserted on the screen.

5. In the resulting box, type the expression **.085*BALANCE**. The asterisk symbol indicates multiplication.

6. To place this field in the view, press F5

7. In response to the prompt *Enter field name* type **C_CHARGE**. This is the name you are assigning to this field. You could use any valid field name except one already used for something else.

This calculated field is placed in the view, and your screen will look like Figure 6-9.

Figure 6-9
A calculated field

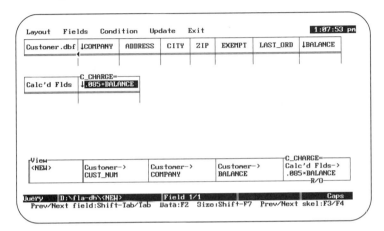

8. Inspect your view with F2 .

If you are interested, you can return to the design screen and filter the records by displaying only those for which the balance is greater than zero (carrying charge is meaningless for 0 balance).

When finished, press Esc and respond with **Y** to abandon. You do not need to save this query.

Combining Data from Two Files in a View

One of the cornerstones of database systems is the ability to combine data from two or more files. For instance, INVOICE contains one record for each invoice; it is tied to a particular customer by the customer-number field. What if you wanted to print a report listing each customer and the invoices for that customer? For this you would need data from both the CUSTOMER and IN-VOICE files, as follows.

1. From the Control Center, make certain the CUSTOMER file is open.

2. Create a new query. Press F5 to remove all fields from the view.

3. From the menu select *Layout / Add file to query*.

4. From the pop-up list of files, select INVOICE. Now you have the two file skeletons shown in Figure 6-10. Note that the field CUST_NUM is common to both of these files. This common field is critical to linking the files together.

Figure 6-10

Two file skeletons on the query design screen

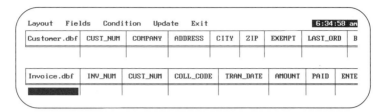

5. The highlight is in the INVOICE (Invoice.dbf) skeleton. Move to the CUST_NUM field and type **LINK** (it can be either upper- or lower-case).

6. Press F4 to move to the CUSTOMER (Customer.dbf) skeleton, move the highlight to CUST_NUM, and type **LINK**

You now have the same entry in the CUST_NUM field of both file skeletons; this causes records of CUSTOMER with a given invoice number to be associated with records of INVOICE with the same invoice number. Note that *LINK* is not a special code; you could use any word (your name for instance) so long as it is entered in both skeletons. With these two files linked, now add fields to the view.

7. From CUSTOMER select CUST_NUM to the view by moving the highlight to CUST_NUM and pressing F5.

8. Select COMPANY to the view.

9. Switch to the INVOICE file by pressing F4.

10. Select to the view (in order) INV_NUM, TRAN_DATE, AMOUNT, and PAID.

To make this view useful for reporting, you will need to have the records in sequence by customer number and then by invoice number. In this way records for each customer will be grouped together.

11. In the CUSTOMER skeleton (use F4) move the highlight to CUST_NUM. You already have the entry LINK. Move the cursor to the space following the *K* and type **,ASC1.** The entry will then be

LINK,ASC1

12. Move to the INVOICE skeleton and enter **ASC2** under the INV_NUM field.

Your query design screen should appear as shown in Figure 6-11.

13. With F2 take a look at your view through the browse screen. Satisfy yourself that the records are indeed in the desired order. Notice that this is a *ReadOnly* view. Then return to the design screen with Shift-F2.

Figure 6-11
The completed
CUSTOMER-
INVOICE
query screen

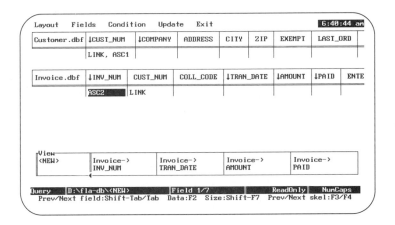

14. Use *Exit/Save changes and exit* or Ctrl-End to complete this exercise.

15. When prompted for the query name, type **CUST_INV**

dBASE proceeds to compile the code needed for this view. When it is finished, you are returned to the Control Center. You will use the query you have just completed (CUST_INV) in the next lesson to generate an invoice report.

■ SUMMARY OF COMMANDS

Topic or Feature	Command Sequence or Key	Page
Add file to query	*Layout/Add file to query*	80
Add/remove view fields	F5	71
Calculated field	*Fields/Create calculated field*	79
Display view data	F2	72
Indexes	*Fields/Include indexes*	78
Next/previous skeleton	F4 / F3	81
Sort on field	*Fields/Sort on this field*	72, 78

■ REVIEW QUESTIONS

1. What is the difference between a *file skeleton* and a *view skeleton*?

2. What action does F5 perform on the query design screen?

3. Give examples of how you would designate character, logical, and date data on a query.

4. In a file skeleton you see query conditions on two different fields on the same line. What does that mean?

5. In a file skeleton you see query conditions on two different fields on different lines. What does that mean?

6. Under the BALANCE field in the CUSTOMER file skeleton you see the entry >=100, <200. What is the condition for filtering records?

7. What is the difference between the query condition **"ABC*"** and **"*ABC*"**?

8. What is the difference between an ASCII sort and a dictionary sort?

9. What is the difference between indexing and sorting?

10. You see the entry *ReadOnly* in the status bar of a view. What does this mean?

11. How do you indicate that records of a view are to be displayed in ascending ASCII sequence based on a particular field?

12. Before two files can be linked, they must have something in common. Explain.

■ *HANDS-ON EXERCISES*

Exercise 6-1

Using INVOICE, create a view that includes all invoice records that meet the following conditions.

Entered by Jack or Alice (condition on ENTERED_BY)

The amount paid is less than the invoice amount (use a condition on PAID)

The records must be in order by ENTERED_BY and then by INV_NUM. Save the view as INV_SPEC. Use Quick Report to print a report from this view.

Exercise 6-2

Using the CUSTOMER and INVOICE files, create a view that includes all invoice records that are not paid in full. (The condition is that the PAID field is less than the AMOUNT field.) Output is to be in Invoice-number order and must include the following fields.

Invoice number

Company name

Transaction date

Invoice amount

Invoice balance (Invoice amount minus paid amount)

Save the view as CUS_INV2. Use Quick Report to print a report.

Exercise 6-3   Using the BIKERS file, create a view named STAT_D that includes all records with a STATUS field value of *D*. The output must be in order by the fields CLUB, LAST, and FIRST and must include the following fields.

Biker number

Last name

First name

Club

Races

Best

Points

Exercise 6-4   For this assignment you will need a new data file containing results of bike racers' finishes. This file, to be named RACES, must include three fields: NBA_NUM, character, length 4; FINISH, numeric, length 2; and POINTS, numeric, length 2. Enter the following 17 records into the file.

NBA_NUM	FINISH	POINTS	NBA_NUM	FINISH	RPOINTS
2006	8	7	1150	4	11
1150	1	16	3910	3	12
2006	11	4	1609	8	7
2829	6	9	1609	10	5
2006	8	7	1150	2	14
1609	7	8	2006	9	6
3910	4	11	2829	8	7
2829	14	1	1150	1	16
1609	8	7	1150	3	12
2829	9	6	2006	13	2
1609	6	9	3901	5	10
1150	2	14	2829	6	9
1609	6	9	3910	2	14
2829	7	8			

Create a view named RESULTS consisting of the following fields.

From BIKERS: NBA_NUM, LAST, FIRST, CLUB

From RACES: FINISH, RPOINTS

Sequencing must be on CLUB, LAST, and FIRST. Use Quick Report to print a report.

SEVEN Report Generation

OBJECTIVES

In this lesson you will learn how to:

- Enter descriptive information into the report design screen.
- Enter data fields into the report design screen.
- Generate reports with header lines at the beginning of each page of the report.
- Generate reports with summary lines at the end of the report.
- Include subtotals for individual groups of records in a file.
- Generate a customer invoice report using data from two files via the CUST_INV view you created.

A BASIC REPORT

Features of a Typical Report

Since Lesson 2 you have used the Quick Report feature to generate printed output. Although convenient to use, it gives you little versatility. In contrast, the report design capabilities of dBASE allow you to create your own report formats with a wide variety of options. Actually, defining a report format is similar to designing a dBASE form: from a report design screen you define exactly what you want. Take a look at the typical report shown in Figure 7-1 (which you will generate in the first exercise).

The Report Design Screen

This report consists of three parts. First is the **page header** which contains information printed at the top of each page of the report. Although this report does not include one, reports can also have a corresponding **page footer**, information printed at the bottom of each page. For instance, you will sometimes see the page number printed in the page footer rather than in the page

Figure 7-1
The customer
address report

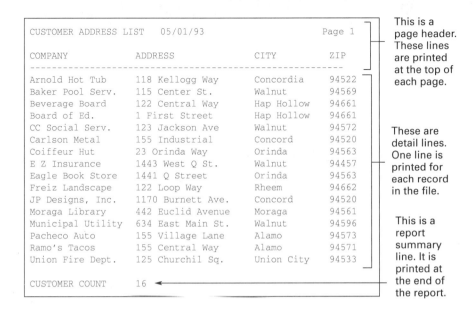

```
CUSTOMER ADDRESS LIST    05/01/93                        Page 1

COMPANY            ADDRESS           CITY        ZIP
-----------------------------------------------------------
Arnold Hot Tub     118 Kellogg Way   Concordia   94522
Baker Pool Serv.   115 Center St.    Walnut      94569
Beverage Board     122 Central Way   Hap Hollow  94661
Board of Ed.       1 First Street    Hap Hollow  94661
CC Social Serv.    123 Jackson Ave   Walnut      94572
Carlson Metal      155 Industrial    Concord     94520
Coiffeur Hut       23 Orinda Way     Orinda      94563
E Z Insurance      1443 West Q St.   Walnut      94457
Eagle Book Store   1441 Q Street     Orinda      94563
Freiz Landscape    122 Loop Way      Rheem       94662
JP Designs, Inc.   1170 Burnett Ave. Concord     94520
Moraga Library     442 Euclid Avenue Moraga      94561
Municipal Utility  634 East Main St. Walnut      94596
Pacheco Auto       155 Village Lane  Alamo       94573
Ramo's Tacos       155 Central Way   Alamo       94571
Union Fire Dept.   125 Churchil Sq.  Union City  94533

CUSTOMER COUNT     16 ◀
```

This is a page header. These lines are printed at the top of each page.

These are detail lines. One line is printed for each record in the file.

This is a report summary line. It is printed at the end of the report.

header, as in this example. Following the page header are **detail lines,** which represent the body of the report. The **report summary** portion of the report is exactly what the name suggests: one or more lines that summarize the report. In this example, the report summary indicates how many records from the file were printed.

The layout for a report such as the one in Figure 7-1 is defined through the report design screen shown in Figure 7-2. As you can see, this design screen is similar to the other design screens. It includes a menu bar at the top and a status bar and navigation line at the bottom. It also has a ruler beneath the menu bar that shows column positions, margin settings, and tab settings.

Indicates column in which cursor is located

Figure 7-2
The report design
screen

Band border
Band
Cursor is here

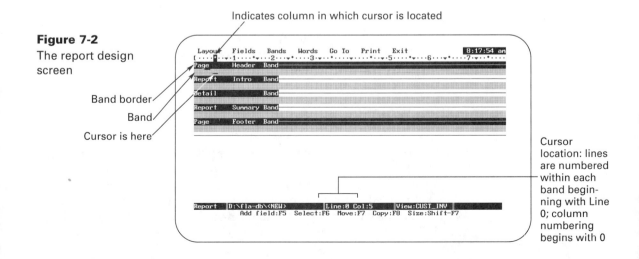

Cursor location: lines are numbered within each band beginning with Line 0; column numbering begins with 0

Whereas the form design screen consists of one large layout surface, the report design screen is divided into five separate areas (corresponding to report needs) called **bands**. For instance, it is within the **Page Header Band** that you define what you want printed for the page header. Notice that the page header of the report in Figure 7-1 consists of four lines of output. There are also bands corresponding to the other three portions of the report: the **Detail Band**, the **Report Summary Band**, and the **Page Footer Band**. In addition, there is one other band called the **Report Intro Band**, in which you can define information to be printed on only the first page of the report. Notice the distinction in Figure 7-2 between the band border and the band itself (which is shaded) located directly beneath the border. Here each band consists of one line. However, you can open up a band to as many lines as you like—the Page Header Band of Figure 7-1 consists of four lines. If a band border has no band area, that band will not be included in a report.

Now bring up an empty report design screen with the following sequence of steps and do some exploring.

1. Open the CUSTOMER data file.

2. From the Reports panel select <create>; get rid of the resulting menu with (Esc).

   Your screen should look like Figure 7-2.

3. Move the cursor around in the screen; notice that the *Line/Col* indicators of the status bar change.

4. Position the cursor anywhere in the Report Intro Band border (not in the band itself, but the border).

5. Press (Enter), and the band disappears (the border remains). This deletes the report intro from the ensuing report. Press (Enter) again, and the band reappears. In this case, (Enter) serves as a toggle. Press (Enter) again to delete this band, as you will not use it for this exercise.

6. Delete the Page Footer Band.

7. Move the cursor to the Page Header Band. Press (Enter) five times; the area is opened to six lines.

8. From Figure 7-1 you know that this portion of the report requires four lines, so you must delete two of them. Move the cursor so that it is not in the last line of the six band lines. Delete one line with (Ctrl)-(Y).

An alternate to this key combination for deleting (or adding) lines is the menu system. Access the *Words* option of the menu bar. Experiment with the *Add line* and *Remove line* commands. When finished, make certain that you have four lines in the header band. Use whichever method for adding and removing lines appeals to you.

The goal of this exercise is to produce a report definition for the report shown in Figure 7-1. When you are finished, your design screen will look like Figure 7-3.

Figure 7-3
The completed
customer address
report design screen

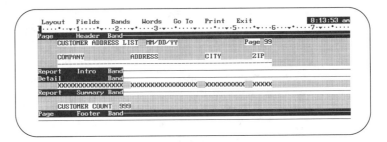

Entering Data Fields

As with the form design screen, fields must be entered into the report design screen exactly where you want them printed. Begin by designating the fields that will be included in the Detail Band.

1. Move the cursor to column 5 of the single-line detail band.

2. From the *Fields* menu select *Add field*.

    The pop-up menu shown in Figure 7-4 appears; the first column displays the fields of CUSTOMER. Select COMPANY.

Figure 7-4
The *Add field*
pop-up menu

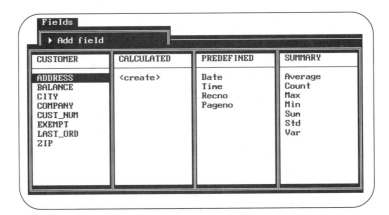

3. The resulting pop-up menu allows you to change formatting for this field. You can accept the definition as shown, so press Ctrl-End to place this field on the layout surface.

    You will see a row of X's representing the COMPANY field.

4. Use → to move the cursor so that there are two shaded spaces to the left of the cursor. (Refer to Figure 7-3.) *Do not use the spacebar* to move the cursor because that will cause the COMPANY field and the one you are about to designate (ADDRESS) to be treated as a single entity, resulting in confusing output.

5. Insert the ADDRESS field in the same way you inserted COMPANY. Then repeat the process for the CITY and ZIP fields.

This completes the Detail Band. One other observation is significant: A single line of the Detail Band results in the printed output being single-spaced. If this band had included a second line (blank), the output would be double-spaced.

Entering Descriptions

Next enter the descriptive information required for this report, which includes entries in both the Page Header and Report Summary bands. Although the widths of bands can be adjusted at any time during screen work, the results can be confusing to a beginner. It is a little less confusing if you set the number of lines in a band before beginning entry. So before you begin, make certain the Page Header Band consists of 4 lines.

1. Move the cursor to position 5 of the first line (line 0) of the Page Header Band; the position indicator in the status bar should read *Line:0 Col:5*. (The line counter in the status bar displays the line number starting with 0 for each band.)

2. Type the heading **CUSTOMER ADDRESS LIST** then use → to move to position 53 and type **Page** (ignore the date field for now).

3. Move the cursor to line 2, position 5 (down two lines and to the left). Type the column-heading line as shown in Figure 7-3.

4. Move down to the last line of this band and type the row of hyphens.

5. Move the cursor to the Report Summary Band. If you do not already have two lines in this band, add one now.

6. Position the cursor on line 1 (the second line), position 5, of this band. Type **CUSTOMER COUNT**

Other Types of Entries

In the report of Figure 7-1 you see other information not available from the data file. The first line includes the date the report was run and a page number; the last line indicates the total number of records processed. These features are available from the *Fields/Add field* menu.

1. Move the cursor to the first line of the Page Header Band so that there are two spaces following the word *LIST* (see Figure 7-3).

2. Select the *Add field* option of the *Fields* menu. The pop-up menu shown in Figure 7-4 appears.

3. From the *PREDEFINED* column select *Date*. Since the format does not need to be changed, press Ctrl-End to place this selection on the layout surface.

4. Move the cursor so that it is to the right of the description *Page* on the screen. From the menu select *Fields / Add field*, then select *Pageno*. For this field, you must change the *Template*. Move to that option, press Enter, change the entry to **99**, and press Enter again to complete the operation. Press Ctrl-End to the place this selection on the layout surface.

5. Move the cursor so that it is separated by two spaces from the word *COUNT* in the Report Summary Band. Repeat step 4, this time selecting *Count* from the *SUMMARY* column and making the *Template* **999**. This will give you a count of the number of records processed for the detail lines of the report. Complete the operation with Ctrl-End.

6. Compare your report design screen to Figure 7-3 and make any appropriate corrections. You can delete descriptions and fields or move sections of the screen exactly as you did in forms design.

7. When finished, use *Exit / Save changes and exit* or press Ctrl-End to save your report definition. In response to the prompt *Save as* type **CUST_ADD** (representing CUSTomer ADDress report).

After dBASE has completed the report generation program you are returned to the Control Center.

Running a Report

To start with a clean slate, terminate dBASE then bring it back up again. To run the report, you must first open the CUSTOMER file, then select CUST_ADD from the Reports panel. However, to obtain the report of Figure 7-1, records of the file must be sequenced in alphabetic order based on the company name. The full set of steps is as follows.

1. Open the CUSTOMER data file.

2. Activate the COMPANY index. Recall from Lesson 5 that you use F2 to display the records, select the *Organize / Order records by index*, and select COMPANY from the list of index fields. Then press Esc to return to the Control Center.

3. Select CUST_ADD from the Reports panel. In response to the pop-up menu, select the *Print report* option.

4. From the resulting pop-up menu, you can look at your report by selecting *View report on screen* or you can print it with *Begin printing*.

When either is completed, you are returned to the Control Center.

. . . .
GROUPING RECORDS IN A REPORT

Group Totals and Group Bands

In Lesson 6 you created the CUST_INV view, which merges information from two data files, CUSTOMER and INVOICE. When you looked at the browse screen or quick report you saw the list of invoices grouped by customer. Using the report generation capabilities of dBASE, you can print a group total report such as the partial one shown in Figure 7-5. This report displays data taken from both files as accessed through the view. Also observe that the last column (Unpaid Balance) is obtained by calculation: Amount Paid is subtracted from Invoice Amount.

Figure 7-5
A report with
group totals

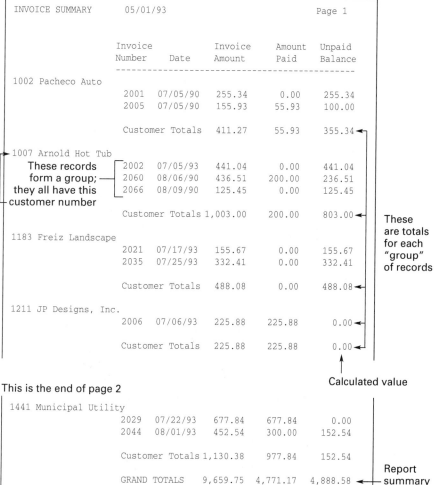

Top portion of page 1

```
INVOICE SUMMARY      05/01/93                            Page 1


                     Invoice           Invoice    Amount   Unpaid
                     Number    Date    Amount     Paid     Balance
                     ------------------------------------------------
1002 Pacheco Auto
                     2001   07/05/90   255.34      0.00    255.34
                     2005   07/05/90   155.93     55.93    100.00

                     Customer Totals   411.27     55.93    355.34

1007 Arnold Hot Tub
   These records     2002   07/05/93   441.04      0.00    441.04
   form a group;     2060   08/06/90   436.51    200.00    236.51
   they all have this 2066  08/09/90   125.45      0.00    125.45
   customer number
                     Customer Totals 1,003.00    200.00    803.00

1183 Freiz Landscape
                     2021   07/17/93   155.67      0.00    155.67
                     2035   07/25/93   332.41      0.00    332.41

                     Customer Totals   488.08      0.00    488.08

1211 JP Designs, Inc.
                     2006   07/06/93   225.88    225.88      0.00

                     Customer Totals   225.88    225.88      0.00
```

These
are totals
for each
"group"
of records

Calculated value

This is the end of page 2

```
1441 Municipal Utility
                     2029   07/22/93   677.84    677.84      0.00
                     2044   08/01/93   452.54    300.00    152.54

                     Customer Totals 1,130.38    977.84    152.54

                     GRAND TOTALS    9,659.75  4,771.17  4,888.58
```

Report
summary
total

This report includes a page header, detail lines, and a report summary line as does the customer address report. However, each group of records (those with the same customer number) is clearly identified. In a sense, each group is analogous to an entire report. That is, each group of records has a group introduction and a group summary which are created by the group bands in the design screen shown in Figure 7-6. The following shows you how to include a group in a report.

Figure 7-6

The design screen with group bands

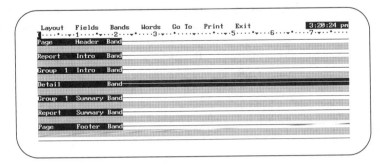

1. From the Control Center Queries panel open CUST_INV.

2. From the Reports panel select *<create>*.

   You should have the basic report design screen overlaid by a pull-down menu.

3. Select *Bands/Add a group band*.

   A short pop-up menu appears with the first entry *Field value* highlighted. Here you must indicate the field on which the records are grouped (the customer number).

4. Press ⌷Enter⌷, and a pop-up menu appears with a list of fields in this view. Select CUST_NUM, and the group bands are inserted as shown in Figure 7-6.

Entering the Basics

The completed design screen that you will build is shown in Figure 7-7. Making the entries for the Page Header, Group 1 Intro, and Detail Bands is no different from procedures you followed in the preceding exercise.

1. Open up the Page Header Band to six lines and proceed to make the entries in exactly the same way you did for the customer address report. Note that, as shown, there are two blank lines between the title line and the first column-heading line. Delete the Report Intro Band.

Figure 7-7
The completed
invoice summary
report design screen

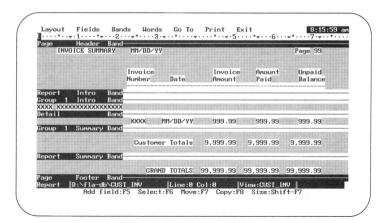

2. For the Group 1 Intro Band entries, move the cursor to the first position of this band. Select *Fields / Add field*. From the resulting list, select CUST_NUM. Press ⌨Enter⌨ and then ⌨Ctrl⌨-⌨End⌨ to place this selection on the layout surface.

3. Move the cursor one position to the right with ⌨→⌨ and repeat the process for the COMPANY field. This completes your entries for this band.

4. Move to the Detail Band and insert the following fields beginning at the indicated columns.

24	INV_NUM
32	TRAN_DATE
45	AMOUNT
56	PAID

5. Now insert the balance field which will be calculated by subtracting PAID from AMOUNT. Move the cursor to position 67 and select *Fields/Add field*.

6. From the *CALCULATE* column select *<create>*.

   A pop-up menu for defining the calculated field appears.

7. Because you will need to refer to this field for group and total summaries, it must have a name. With the highlight on the *Name* menu option, press ⌨Enter⌨, type the name **BALANCE**, and press ⌨Enter⌨ again to complete the operation.

8. For the *Expression* line enter **AMOUNT-BALANCE**

9. Change the *Template* to **999.99**

10. Press ⌨Ctrl⌨-⌨End⌨ to place this selection on the layout surface.

Entering Summary Lines

The remainder of this exercise involves entering summary line information. You will define a summary line that will be printed at the end of each group with totals for that group, and a report summary line with the totals for the entire report. First, do the Group 1 Summary Band entries as follows.

1. Move to this band and open it to three lines. At line 1 (the middle line of the three) type the description **Customer Totals** beginning at position 25.

2. Move to position 43 and from *Fields* select the *Add field* option.

   This output item is to be the sum of the AMOUNT field for records of this customer. Thus your entry will need to be from the *SUMMARY* column of the menu (shown in Figure 7-4).

3. Select the *Sum* entry from the menu.

   The menu shown in Figure 7-8 appears. Notice that the *Operation* entry is defaulted to SUM.

Figure 7-8
The Add field
description pop-up
menu

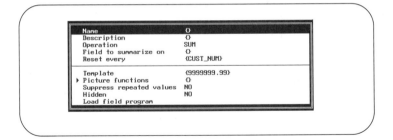

4. Select *Field to summarize on* and a pop-up list of fields appears. Select AMOUNT (you want the total of the AMOUNT fields for this customer).

   The next menu item is *Reset every {CUST_NUM}*. When you opened the band you designated the field controlling the group as CUST_NUM. When the resulting report program is run to generate the report, each record is read and its customer number is compared to that of the preceding record. If they are the same, the value from AMOUNT is added to the amount subtotal. If they are different, the group summary line is printed and the amount subtotal is reset to 0. Leave the *Reset every* default entry unchanged.

5. Move to the *Template* entry and change it to **9,999.99**

6. Press [Ctrl]-[End] to place this selection on the layout surface.

7. Repeat the preceding steps to insert the PAID field summary beginning at position 54.

8. Repeat the preceding steps to insert the BALANCE field beginning at position 65. Note that you will select BALANCE from beneath the *CALCULATED* column of the field list.

The process for making the entries to the Report Summary Band is identical to that for the Group 1 Summary Band. Note that the numeric field templates are larger to provide for the potentially larger totals of all records in the file. Also, you will see *Reset every < REPORT >* in the menu of Figure 7-8. This is the report grand total, so you do not want it set to 0 for each new group. When you are finished, press Ctrl-End to save the report form; use the name CUST_INV (for CUSTomer INVoice).

Once back at the Control Center, run the report. Check the output via the screen and then print a copy.

■ *SUMMARY OF COMMANDS*

Topic of Features	Command Sequence or Key	Page
Insert a band line	Enter or *Words / Add line*	87
Insert a data field	F5 or *Fields / Add field*	88
Insert a group band	*Bands / Add a group band*	92
Print report	*Print / Begin printing*	90
Remove a band line	Ctrl-Y or *Words / Remove line*	87
Save report design	*Exit / Save changes and exit* or	90
	Layout / Save this report	
Select segment of screen	F6	
View report on screen	*Print / View report on screen*	90

■ *REVIEW QUESTIONS*

1. What is the difference between a band and a band border?

2. What does it mean if a band border is not followed by any band lines?

3. What is the difference between a page header and a page footer?

4. What is a detail line?

5. What would the output of a report look like if the Detail Band of Figure 7-3 consisted of the line shown plus two blank lines?

6. How would you move the ZIP code field farther to the right in the Detail Band of Figure 7-3?

7. What do group bands allow you to do?

8. Why are the group total numeric fields defined larger than the individual fields they represent? For instance, the Invoice Amount field is defined as 999.99 but the corresponding group total field is defined as 9,999.99.

■ HANDS-ON EXERCISES

Exercise 7-1   Using the BIKERS file create a report to include the following.

Page header: three of four lines with the title BIKER'S RACE SUMMARY; include the date the report is run and a page number

Detail: the following fields: Last name, First name, Membership number, Number of races, and Points

Report summary: total Number of races and total Points

The output must be in sequence by Last name then by First name.

Exercise 7-2   Using the BIKERS file create a report with group totals on the CLUB field. The output for the first record must appear as follows (note that an asterisk is included following the group totals). The report summary must include totals on these same two fields with an ** indication.

```
           CLUB RACING SUMMARY     05/03/93            Page 1

CLUB                 CLUB MEMBER              RACES   POINTS
==============       =====================    =====   ======
Felines
                     Baur      Kirstin          5       26
                     Yancy     Gloria           6       40
                     Alton     Joanne           5       36
                     Zucker    Ida              7       75
                     O'Conner  Laura            6       84
                     Porter    Kyle             4       46
                               CLUB TOTALS     33*     307*
```

Exercise 7-3   Use the query RACE_SUM (from Lesson 6) to create a report with group totals on the field NBA_NUM. The output for the first record must appear as
follows. Note that the Finish and Points values are derived from data in the
view taken from the RACES data file. The report summary must include a
total on the Points field.

```
                                                          Page No. 1


                              RACING SUMMARY REPORT    05/01/93
            Member
            Number    Last Name    First Name    Club

            1150      Kimball      Gale          Roadrunners    Finish   Points
                                                                  1        16
                                                                  2        14
                                                                  4        11
                                                                  2        14
                                                                  1        16
                                                                  3        12
                                                                          ---
                                                      RACERS POINTS       83
```

LESSON **EIGHT**

Form Letters and Labels

OBJECTIVES

In this lesson you will learn how to:

- Include database information in creating a form letter.
- Enter and edit text in a form letter.
- Create and print mailing labels.

CREATING FORM LETTERS

The Concepts of Mailmerge

You are undoubtedly familiar with form letters: those very personalized messages sent *only* to you—and thousands of others. Through a combination of database and word processing capabilities, preparing form letters is a simple task. To find out how it is done, you will prepare the form letter shown in Figure 8-1 for mailing to all companies in the CUSTOMER file.

Figure 8-1
A typical form letter

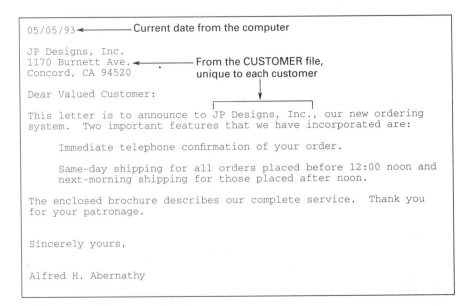

```
05/05/93 ◄──────── Current date from the computer

JP Designs, Inc.
1170 Burnett Ave. ◄─────── From the CUSTOMER file,
Concord, CA 94520          unique to each customer

Dear Valued Customer:

This letter is to announce to JP Designs, Inc., our new ordering
system.  Two important features that we have incorporated are:

      Immediate telephone confirmation of your order.

      Same-day shipping for all orders placed before 12:00 noon and
      next-morning shipping for those placed after noon.

The enclosed brochure describes our complete service.  Thank you
for your patronage.


Sincerely yours,


Alfred H. Abernathy
```

Actually, you are already familiar with most of the commands required to prepare form letters. This capability is an option of report generation called **mailmerge**, the ability to merge a text document with addresses stored in a database. When you access the mailmerge option, you are presented with the familiar report design screen consisting of the five basic report bands. However, all bands except the detail band are closed, and the detail band consists of several lines as shown in Figure 8-2. Note that this area is not shaded as are bands of the report design screen. Actually, this design screen is used much differently than the corresponding work surface of the report design screen. That is, you have at your disposal a very basic word processor. You can, for example, set margins, indent paragraphs, and not worry about pressing Enter as you approach the right margin while typing text. When the right margin is reached, dBASE automatically progresses to the next line. This feature is called **word wrap**. The only time you press Enter is to end a paragraph. As you will see, dBASE treats each block of text terminated with Enter as a separate paragraph. This means that the three lines of address information in the letter of Figure 8-1 constitute three paragraphs.

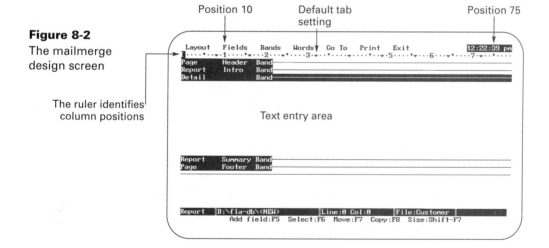

Figure 8-2
The mailmerge design screen

The ruler identifies column positions

The line just below the menu bar is called the **ruler**. The single digits represent column positions: 1 signifies column 10, 2 signifies 20, and so on. The upside-down triangles indicate the default tab settings. The [character at the left indicates the left margin.

The Mailmerge Design Screen

To find out how this works, create a mailmerge form to generate the letter of Figure 8-1 as follows.

1. From the Control Center open the CUSTOMER file.

2. From the Reports panel select <*create*>. A design screen overlaid by the *Layout* menu appears.

3. From the *Layout* menu, select *Quick layouts/Mailmerge layout*. The mailmerge design screen of Figure 8-2 is displayed.

4. Move the cursor down to the first line of the Detail Band. With → attempt to move the cursor to the right.

Notice that the cursor moves down instead of to the right. The only area of the mailmerge Detail Band to which you can move the cursor is area into which you have entered text. If you use the spacebar the cursor will move to the right as you enter spaces (text) into the work surface.

Setting Margins

Before entering text, you should first set your margins. For this letter you will use 1-inch margins. With 8½″ by 11″ paper, the margins will be at 1 inch and 7½ inches (referring to the ruler in Figure 8-2, the settings will be 10 and 75). Margin settings can be confusing at first because the mailmerge editor allows you to set separate margins for each paragraph. Each line in the Detail Band of Figure 8-2 is treated by the editor as a separate paragraph with default margins of 0 and 254. The simplest approach is to delete all detail lines except one, set your margins of 10 and 75, then reopen the Detail Band.

1. Position the cursor on the first detail line and successively press Delete until only one line remains.

2. Select the *Words/Modify ruler* menu option.

   The cursor is positioned on the ruler.

3. Move the cursor to ruler position 10 (the 1 marked on the ruler—refer to Figure 8-2). Notice that the column number in the status bar does not change to reflect the cursor position on the ruler.

4. Type the character [to indicate the position of the left margin, then press Ctrl -End to complete this action.

   Control is returned to the mailmerge design screen. The left-bracket character [should be displayed at position 10.

5. Repeat steps 2–4, this time setting the right margin with] at position 75 (refer to Figure 8-2).

   The right-bracket character] should be displayed at position 75.

If you like, you may press Enter several times to open up the Detail Band, although this is not necessary. New lines are automatically inserted by the editor as you need them.

Entering Variable Information

The first entries to make are those that can vary from one letter to another: the date (which depends upon when the letter is printed) and the addressee.

1. Position the cursor at the top left of the mailmerge design screen.

   If you set the margins properly, this should be line 0, column 10. If not, reset your margins.

2. From the menu select *Fields/Add field*. From the resulting menu select *Date* from the *PREDEFINED* column.

3. Since there is no change required to the pop-up field description menu, press Ctrl-End to place this entry on the layout surface.

4. Press End to move the cursor to the end of this field then press Enter twice to leave one blank line following the date entry.

5. From the menu select *Fields/Add field* and insert the COMPANY field.

6. On successive lines, insert the ADDRESS and CITY fields.

7. Move the cursor to the right of the CITY field template and type a comma, a space, the letters **CA**, and two spaces. (Since the data file does not include a field for state, assume that all companies are in the state of California.)

   When finished, your cursor should be at line 4, column 26.

8. Insert the ZIP field.

   Your screen should look like Figure 8-3. If you have any significant differences, simply delete the offending field and reenter it.

Figure 8-3
Date and addressee entries

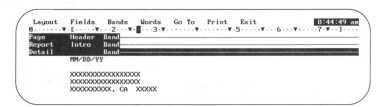

Entering Text

So far you can see that working with the mailmerge design screen requires many of the same techniques as the other layout surfaces. The next step of this example is to enter the text of the letter using the dBASE editor. Refer to Figure 8-1 as you work.

1. After entering the ZIP field, press ⟨Enter⟩ twice to move the cursor to line 6. Type the greeting **Dear Valued Customer:** then press ⟨Enter⟩ twice to insert a blank line before the body of the letter.

2. Type the first portion of the first sentence:

   This letter is to announce to

3. At this point, you must insert the company name. Make certain there is a space following the word *to* then access the *Fields/Add field* menu and select the field COMPANY. Press ⟨Ctrl⟩-⟨End⟩.

   Your line will appear as follows.

   This letter is to announce to XXXXXXXXXXXXXXXXX

4. Leave one space following the last X and resume typing the text. When you reach the right margin the cursor automatically jumps to a new line.

5. Continue typing until you have entered the complete letter.

   Your screen should look like Figure 8-4. Be sure to insert blank lines as shown. Also, notice that the two middle paragraphs are not indented as they are in Figure 8-1. You will take care of this next by resetting the margins.

Figure 8-4
Completed text entry

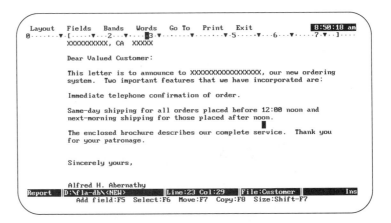

6. Position the cursor anywhere in the third paragraph (begins with *Same-day shipping*).

7. From the menu select *Words/Modify ruler*. Move the cursor to position 15 (between 2 and 3 on the ruler) and type [. Complete the action with ⟨Ctrl⟩-⟨End⟩.

   You are returned to the mailmerge design screen, and this paragraph is indented.

8. Position the cursor anywhere in the paragraph beginning with the word *Immediate* and repeat step 7.

Saving and Viewing the Letter

Before doing anything further, you should save this letter.

1. Select *Layout/Save this report*.

2. In response to the prompt *Save as* type a descriptive file name, for instance, M_CU_ORD (CU_ORD for CUstomer ORDer letter). If you use *M_* as the first two characters of all mailmerge documents, they will be easily recognizable on the Reports panel display.

With the design safely saved, proofread it to make certain that everything is correct. Use the arrow keys to move around and [Delete] and [Backspace] to delete text or field templates. Notice that the navigation line indicates you can select, move, and delete text just as you did in the form design screen.

To inspect your work, select *Print/View report on screen*. When you are satisfied, you can terminate this session through the *Exit* menu. If you want to print the form letter, remember that you will be printing one page for each record in the file. Since the ZB_CUST (zero balance customers) query consists of only five records, you may wish to use it. If so, use the following sequence.

1. From the Control Center open the ZB_CUST query.

2. Highlight M_CU_ORD (or whatever name you used for your mailmerge document) in the Reports panel.

3. Press [Enter] then select the print option.

4. From the resulting pop-up menu select *Begin printing*.

When printing is completed, you are returned to the Control Center.

. . . .
CREATING LABELS

In addition to form letters that use information stored in a database, dBASE also allows you to print labels. From the Labels panel you can design forms that allow you to print mailing labels, name badges, and even addresses on envelopes. Typical computer-generated labels are shown in Figure 8-5. These are standard size: 1″ high and 3½″ wide (the height is commonly referred to as 15/16 because of the space between the labels). They are available on single-column format, as shown, and also with two and three labels across. dBASE accommodates all of these formats and many more. Now create a label form for the CUSTOMER file.

Figure 8-5
Sample labels

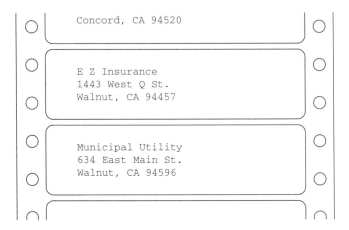

1. From the Control Center, make certain CUSTOMER is open in the Data panel. Then select *<create>* from the Labels panel.

   The label design screen shown in Figure 8-6 appears.

Figure 8-6
The label
design screen

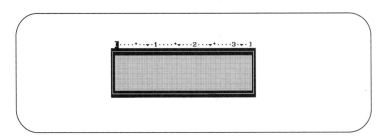

2. You are looking at the standard 15/16" by 3½" label design screen, which you will use for this exercise. However, to give you an idea of the options you have, select from the menu *Dimensions/Predefined size*; the resulting list of options is shown in Figure 8-7. Press Esc to return to the label design screen.

3. Move the cursor to line 1, column 3, the point at which you will begin label definition. To insert the company name field, select from the menu *Fields/Add field*.

4. From the resulting list of fields, select COMPANY. Press Ctrl - End to exit from the field description menu and complete this entry.

5. As you can see, this procedure is identical to those you used in designing forms and reports. Proceed to enter the ADDRESS and CITY fields on the following two lines.

Figure 8-7
Label size options

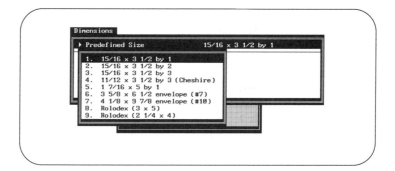

6. As you did with the form letter, type a comma, a space, the letters **CA**, and two spaces. Then insert the ZIP field. When you are finished, your label design should look like Figure 8-8(a).

Figure 8-8(a)
The completed label design screen

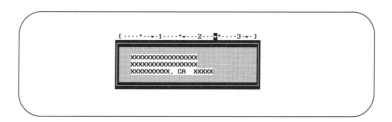

Figure 8-8(b)
An incorrect version of the label design

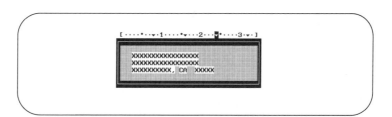

Compare Figure 8-8(a) (correct) with Figure 8-8(b) (not correct). Notice in (a) that there is no shading surrounding CA. You can check the difference in these two after you save your label.

7. Save your work with *Layout/Save this label design*. Use CUST_ADD for the label name.

8. View the results of your work by selecting *Print/View labels on screen*. Notice that for each label, CA is separated from the comma by one space.

To observe the effect of not including the spaces surrounding CA, modify your label so that it looks like Figure 8-8(b). For this, position the cursor immediately following the comma and press ⌊Delete⌋ repeatedly to delete everything to the right. Then use ⌊→⌋ to position the cursor, and reenter **CA** and the ZIP field to produce the label shown in Figure 8-8(b). Use *Print/View labels on screen* to inspect the results. You can see that CA remains fixed in its position, leaving numerous spaces for city names that do not fill the allotted number of positions. Since you do not want to save this label, press ⌊Esc⌋.

As with the form letter, if you want printed output, you can use the ZB_CUST query to limit the amount of printing.

■ *SUMMARY OF COMMANDS*

Topic or Feature	Command Sequence or Key	Page
Create mailmerge document	Layout/Quick layouts/ Mailmerge layout	100
Insert a data field	Fields/Add field	101
Save a report	Layout/Save this report	103
Select label size	Dimensions/Predefined size	104
Set margins	Words/Modify ruler	100

■ *REVIEW QUESTIONS*

1. The action of the dBASE editor automatically progressing to the next line when the current line becomes full during text entry is called

   _____.

2. What is the difference between the Detail Band of the report design screen and the mailmerge design screen?

3. Which code characters signify left and right margins?

4. In the completed form letter design of Figure 8-4 the second and third paragraphs are indented from the left to set them off from the others. How would you include an equal indention from the right?

5. What would you do to the label design of Figure 8-8(a) if you wanted the label addressed with the following? *Attn: Purchasing*

■ *HANDS-ON EXERCISES*

Exercise 8-1   Using the BIKERS file, design a screen to print the following form letter. The shaded areas represent data from the file; the date is taken from the dBASE date function. To avoid excessive printing, define a query that includes only those records with *H* for the STATUS field. Print the report using that view.

```
To: Gale Kimball
From: Race Chairperson
Subject: Race standings
Date: 05/05/93

As you are well aware, this has been a busy season with a variety
of races. We have thoroughly enjoyed working with you and the
other members of the Roadrunners Club. Our records include the
following summary of your participation.

    Number of races you have ridden: 6
    Total points earned: 83

If this does not agree with your own records, please give us a
call. Yours for great biking.

Jean
```

Exercise 8-2   Using the BIKERS file, design a screen to print the following name tags (labels). The shaded areas represent data from the file. To avoid excessive printing, define a query that includes only those records with *H* for the STATUS field. Print the report using that view.

```
HI!! I'm
    Gale Kimball
        (NBA #1150)

Home club: Roadrunners
```

Answers to Review Questions

LESSON 1

1. Hold down (Shift), press (F2), then release (Shift).

2. Control Center, dot prompt

3. Menu bar, catalog line, panels, file information lines, and navigation line

4. Obtain help by pressing (F1)

5. (F10)

6. (Esc)

7. As a general rule there is none. However, you should be careful of (Esc) because its incorrect use can lose data. Usually (but not always) you are warned and you must confirm with a **Y** for Yes. There are cases in which (Esc) causes you to lose a small amount of data with no warning. These will be brought to your attention in the appropriate lesson.

LESSON 2

1. Character, numeric, float, date, logical, and memo

2. Driver's license number: character; Driver's age: numeric (however, birthdate is more meaningful to store, as age changes each birthday); Person's birthdate: date; Automobile type: character; ZIP Code: character; Club member: logical; Membership in club A, B, or C: character; Mileage: numeric

3. Logical and date are fixed in width (1 and 8). Numeric depends upon the number of digits to be stored. Character also depends on the number of characters in the data. For instance, Social Security number (if hyphens included) would be 11. Names, such as those of people and cities, are a judgment call.

4. When you create a file, you define the structure. The finished product is a file with all fields fully described but with no data. Entering records—actual keying of data—can be done only after the file is defined.

5. (F10)

6. Edit, browse

7. To provide you with descriptive information about the currently open file.

8. Highlight CUSTOMER in the Data panel, press (F2), and select the menu option *Records/Add records*.

LESSON 3

1. In case you make a serious mistake and destroy data, you can always go back to the backup copy.

2. Unless you make these changes in two independent modification actions, you will lose the data in the field of the name change.

3. Overtype causes a newly entered character to replace the character at the position of the cursor. Insert causes a newly entered character to be inserted in front of existing characters.

4. The undo works only if you have not moved to another record since making the change.

5. No, the *Size field* option changes only the width of the display on the current use of the browse screen.

6. One or more fields on the left remain fixed and the rest of the fields scroll when the cursor is moved to the right.

7. The designated field is the only one that can be edited.

8. The action is exactly as described: "The record is marked for deletion." Marked records can be made "invisible" to processing. This way, if the user decides to reactivate a record, it need only be unmarked and not reentered in its entirety.

9. With the *Erase marked records* option of the *Organize* menu or with the PACK command from the dot prompt.

LESSON 4

1. The INVOICE. SCR contains the actual screen definition. The .FMT and .FMO files are program code generated from the SCR file.

2. A calculated field is a form display item that is obtained from calculations using values from fields of the data record.

3. The form is essentially a "window" through which you can view any or all fields from a record. You design the form to suit the needs of a given application. You can display as few or as many of the fields from a record as is required for that particular application.

4. You select a section of the screen to: (1) move it, (2) copy it, or (3) delete it.

5. Move the cursor to one end (or corner) of the section to be selected; press F6 (*Select*); move the cursor to the other end (or opposite corner) of the section to be selected; press Enter.

6. Changing the template affects only the way in which the data is displayed through the form. It has no effect on the data file structure.

7. Upper-case conversion: ! Digits only: 9

8. <ABC>23–xyz, <AB7>51–XYZ, <A/7>34–X82

9. The *Multiple choice* option is used with fields for which there is a discrete (usually relatively small) number of entries that can be made, for example, the four choices for Collection code. This Amount paid field can be any value up to the amount of the invoice.

10. A default value is the value automatically displayed for that field during data entry. It can be accepted by pressing Enter or a new value can be typed in.

11. Set the *Permit edit* option to *No* for every displayed field.

LESSON 5

1. Natural, physical, logical

2. MDX

3. In searching, uppercase and lowercase letters are treated differently. For instance, a search for *Smith* will not find *SMITH*.

4. The customer-number field is character and the amount field is numeric. A special action must be taken to combine a character and a numeric field for indexing.

5. 47

6. You have not activated an index.

7. An index search is much faster than a record search.

8. The non-indexed record search method provides greater versatility in designating the search string.

9. The wildcard characters are used in the search string to indicate "anything can be here." The ? operates on a one-to-one basis and the * indicates anything from no characters at all to any number.

LESSON 6

1. The file skeleton lists the "input" elements to the view; it is a list of fields in the data file. The view skeleton represents the "output" elements from the view.

2. F5 adds fields to and removes fields from the view skeleton.

3. Character: "THIS IS CHARACTER" (delimited with quotes)
Logical: .T. (delimited with periods)
Date: {6/9/97} (delimited with curly braces)

4. Two conditions on the same line mean that both conditions must be met; this is an AND condition.

5. Two conditions on different lines mean that either of the conditions may be met for a record to be selected; this is an OR condition.

6. Records selected will have a BALANCE entry equal to or greater than 100 but less than 200.

7. The condition **"ABC*"** will select only those records with ABC as the first three characters of the field. The condition **"*ABC*"** will select records with ABC anywhere in the field.

8. An ASCII sort places lowercase letters after all the uppercase letters. A dictionary sort ignores case.

9. Indexing sequences records of a file by creating an index to the file yielding a logical order without changing the physical order of records in the file. Sorting creates a new file with the records in the desired sequence.

10. *ReadOnly* means that you cannot write (edit or add records) to the file. This results when the view definition causes a temporary data file to be created for the view.

11. Enter the code *asc* (or *asc1*) under that field.

12. In order for two files to be linked they must have a field in common so that records in one file with a given value for that field can be associated with records in the other file with that same value for the field.

LESSON 7

1. The band border identifies the band, the area into which you make entries to define the report.

2. That band will not be used in the report.

3. A page header is information printed at the top of each page of a report. A page footer is information printed at the bottom of each page of a report.

4. A detail line is a line printed from one record of the input file.

5. The report would be triple-spaced (two blank lines between each detail line.

6. You could move this field either by deleting and then reentering it or by using the *Select* (F6) and *Move* (F7).

7. Group bands allow you to print group header lines and subtotals for individual groups of records.

8. The group total is the sum of values in one or more records. Check the sample output in Figure 7-5 to see this. If the file included many more customers, the report total fields would probably be larger.

LESSON 8

1. word wrap

2. The entire screen of report design is "activated"—you can move anywhere and make entries. The mailmerge design screen is essentially a word processing screen—

you can move only to positions that contain existing entries.

3. The character [signifies left margin, and] signifies right margin.

4. Set the right margin at something less than 75, for example, at 70.

5. Insert the text *Attn: Purchasing* on the first line of the label (above the company name).

dBASE IV Version 1.5/2.0 for DOS Reference and Command Summary

Commands without page numbers are not coverec in this book.

Function Keys

Key	Action	Page
F1 (Help)	Display help	3
Shift-F1 (Pick)	Display list of items available for current fill-in	46
F2 (Data)	Shift to browse/edit screen or browse/custom form screen	17, 18, 52
Shift-F2 (Design)	Display the design screens; transfer to query design from another design screen.	46
F3 (Previous)	Move to previous screen (browse/edit), skeleton (query design), or page (Help)	31
Shift-F3 (Find Previous)	Locate previous occurrence of a search string	65
F4 (Next)	Move to next screen (browse/edit), skeleton (query design), or page (Help)	31
Shift-F4 (Find Next)	Locate next occurrence of a search string	65
F5 (Field)	Add field to layout surface; for query, add/remove field from view skeleton	71
Shift-F5 (Find)	Find a specified search string	
F6 (Select)	Select a section of a design surface (text and/or fields)	48
Shift-F6 (Replace)	Replace search string with another string	
F7 (Move)	Move a selected section on a design surface	48
Shift-F7 (Size)	In browse, change the size of design elements and column widths	
F8 (Copy)	Copy a selected section on a design surface	48
Shift-F8 (Ditto)	Copy data from corresponding field of previous record into current field	19
F9 (Zoom)	Enlarge or shrink file skeletons and some data fill-in areas	
Shift-F9 (Quick Report)	Print a quick report from the open data file or query	21
F10 (Menus)	Access menus for current screen	14
Shift-F10 (Macros)	Access macros prompt box	

Cursor Navigation Keys

Key	Movement/Action	Work Surface	Page
→	Right one position		12
←	Left one position		12
↓	Down one line		12
	To next field	Edit	
↑	Up one line		12
	To previous field	Edit	
Ctrl-→	Beginning of next word/field		
Ctrl-←	Beginning of previous word/field		
Page Down	Display next screen	Browse, edit, word wrap, layout	
Page Up	Display previous screen	Browse, edit, word wrap, layout	28
Ctrl-Page Down	End of text	Word wrap	
	Bottom of layout surface	Layout	
	Current field in last record	Browse, edit	31
Ctrl-Page Up	Beginning of text	Word wrap	
	Top of layout surface	Layout	
	Current field in first record	Browse, edit	31
End	End of field	Edit	
	Last field of record	Browse	
	Last text/field on line	Layout	
	Last column of skeleton	Queries	
Home	Beginning of field	Edit	
	Beginning of record	Browse	
	Left margin	Layout	
	First column of skeleton	Queries	
Backspace	Delete preceding character		12
Ctrl-Backspace	Delete previous word	Word wrap, layout	
Tab	Next field	Edit, browse	31
	Next tab stop	Layout, word wrap (if Insert is OFF)	
	Next column	Queries, lists, tables	
	Insert tab character	Word wrap (if Insert is OFF)	
Shift-Tab	Previous field	Edit, browse	31
	Previous tab stop	Layout, word wrap	
	Previous column	Queries, lists, tables	

Key	Movement/Action	Work Surface	Page
Enter	Next field	Browse, edit	
	Next line	Layout, word wrap	
	Break line, move to new line	Layout, word wrap (if Insert is ON)	
Esc	Exit, abandoning changes		6
	Exit Help	Help	4
	Cancel extended selection	Work surfaces	49
Delete	Delete currently selected item		12, 48
Insert	Toggle Insert ON/OFF		32
Ctrl-Home	Move into memo field	Memo field	
Ctrl-End	Save work and exit		47
	Exit memo field	Memo field	
Ctrl-Enter	Save work and remain	Design screens	

Menu Summary

The following is a partial summary of commands grouped within their respective menus. You have used most of these. You should find those you have not used reasonably intuitive based on what you have learned in this book.

Control Center

Catalog

Use a different catalog
Modify catalog name
Edit description of catalog
Add file to catalog
Remove highlighted file from catalog
Change description of catalog

Tools

Settings
Deleted to ON/OFF

Exit

Exit to dot prompt
Quit to DOS

Browse and edit screens

Records

Undo change to record
Add new records
Mark record for deletion/Clear deletion
Record lock

Organize

> *Create new index*
> *Modify existing index*
> *Order records by index*
> *Sort database on field list*
> *Unmark all records*
> *Erase marked records*

Fields (browse only)

> *Lock fields on left*
> *Blank field*
> *Freeze field*
> *Size field*

Go To

> *Top record*
> *Last record*
> *Record number*
> *Skip*
> *Index key search*
> *Forward search*
> *Backward search*
> *Match capitalization*

Exit

> *Exit*
> *Transfer to Query Design*
> *Return to <object> Design*

Database File (structure screen)

Layout

> *Print database structure*
> *Edit database structure*
> *Save this database file structure*

Organize

> *Create new index*
> *Modify existing index*
> *Order records by index*
> *Remove unwanted index tag*
> *Sort database on field list*
> *Unmark all records*
> *Erase marked records*

Append

> *Enter records from keyboard*
> *Append records from dBASE file*

Go To
>   *Top field*
>   *Last field*
>   *Field number*

Exit
>   *Save changes and exit*
>   *Abandon changes and exit*

Forms panel

Layout
>   *Quick layouts*
>   *Box*
>   *Line*
>   *Edit description of form*
>   *Save this form*

Fields
>   *Add field*
>   *Remove field*
>   *Modify field*

Words
>   *Modify ruler*
>   *Add line*
>   *Remove line*
>   *Insert page break*

Go To
>   *Go to line number*
>   *Forward search*
>   *Backward search*
>   *Replace*

Exit
>   *Save changes and exit*
>   *Abandon changes and exit*

Labels panel

Layout
>   *Edit description of label design*
>   *Save this report*

Dimensions
>   *Predefined size*

Fields

    Add field
    Remove field
    Modify field

Words

    Modify ruler
    Add line
    Remove line
    Insert page break

Go To

    Go to line number
    Forward search
    Backward search
    Replace

Print

    Begin printing
    Eject page now
    Generate sample labels
    View report on screen
    Destination

Exit

    Save changes and exit
    Abandon changes and exit

Queries panel

Layout

    Add file to query
    Remove file from query
    Write view as database file
    Edit description of query
    Save this query

Fields

    Add field to view
    Remove field from view
    Create calculated field
    Delete calculated field
    Sort on this field
    Include indexes

Condition

    Add condition box
    Delete condition box

Exit

    Save changes and exit
    Abandon changes and exit

Reports panel

Layout

   Quick layouts
      Column layout
      Form layout
      Mailmerge layout
   Box
   Line
   Edit description of report
   Save this report

Fields

   Add field
   Remove field
   Modify field

Bands

   Add a group band
   Remove a group band

Words

   Modify ruler
   Add line
   Remove line
   Insert page break

Go To

   Go to line number
   Forward search
   Backward search
   Replace
   Match capitalization

Print

   Begin printing
   Eject page now
   View report on screen
   Destination
   Output options
   Page dimensions

Exit

   Save changes and exit
   Abandon changes and exit

Troubleshooting Guide

Following are troubleshooting hints for the most common problems you will encounter. They are grouped by subject, for example, "Using Indexes and Searching." So in using these hints, first look in the appropriate topic area. If you find no reference, look in the following "General" category, as this contains hints that apply to two or more topic areas.

General

1. Most menu sequences and many activities can be aborted without affecting a file by pressing (Esc).

2. If you are unsure of an operation, access a help screen by pressing (F1).

3. When combining fields (performing arithmetic or concatenating), the fields must be of the same type. For instance, you cannot subtract a character field from a numeric field. If you try you will get the error message *Data type mismatch*.

4. A syntax error means that you have constructed an expression incorrectly. For instance, if you entered the calculated field AMOUNT-PAID as AMOUNT?PAID, you would get a syntax error.

5. If you misspell a field name when creating a calculated field or specifying a query condition, you will receive the message *Variable not found*. Correct the spelling of the field name.

6. In switching from one activity to another, you will sometimes access a form, report, or label file without closing an open data file or query. If the open data file or query is not the one associated with the form, report, or label, dBASE calls your attention to the conflict and lists the currently open file and the one associated with the form, report, or label. Be certain to select the proper one.

Modifying the Structure of a File

1. If you intend to modify the structure of a file, be sure to make a backup copy first.

2. If you add or delete fields and change the name of a field during a single structure-modification sequence, you will lose the data in the field with the name change. Do these steps in independent operations.

3. If you delete the wrong field when making a file structure modification, simply abort the operation with Esc and start over.

4. Do not expect to change the width of fields in a data file through the browse screen *Fields/Size field* menu option. This results in only a "current browse session" change in the column widths for displaying the data. It does not change the file.

Editing Records

1. If you use Esc to exit the record you are editing in either the browse or edit screen, changes to that record will not be entered into the file.

2. Packing permanently erases records marked for deletion. Always double-check your marked records before packing a file.

Creating and Using Forms

1. If you have trouble moving an entry when making changes in a form, just delete the entry and then reenter it.

2. When moving the cursor to the right during form design, be sure to use →. Do not use Spacebar.

3. Before activating a form, make certain you have opened the correct file. If you have opened the wrong file, you will probably get the message *Variable not found*.

4. If the cursor jumps over the *Index key search* option of the *Go To* menu, you have forgotten to assign an index. Do this through the *Organize* menu.

5. If records are presented to you in the wrong order, either you have forgotten to activate an index or you have activated the wrong one.

Using Indexes and Searching

1. When searching using an index, if you get a *Not found* message when you are certain you have a correct entry for the search string, consider the following.

   a. Make sure you have designated the correct index.

   b. Check your use of upper/lowercase letters.

   c. Check to see if your search string is long enough to locate the desired record.

2. If you receive a *Not found* message from a forward or backward search when you are certain you have a correct entry for the search string, following are some checks you can make.

   a. Make sure the cursor is on the field for which the search is to be performed.

   b. Remember that you need the entire field value for a record search (or else wildcard forms); only an index search allows the first portion of a field to be used as the search string.

3. If records are not in the desired order in a display or report, make certain that you selected the correct index.

Designing and Using Queries

1. Do not forget to use quotes around your entry for a condition on a character field. Otherwise, you will probably see no filtering of records.

2. If a condition does not result in the proper records being displayed, check that the condition is on the correct field.

3. Always make certain that AND conditions are on the same line and OR conditions are on different lines.

4. Be careful when using relational operators; for instance, it is easy to use <= instead of >= or to use > when you actually need >=.

5. If the order of records is not correct when sorting on two fields, make certain that you identified the primary field with Asc1 and the secondary with Asc2.

Report Generation

1. If a total is not correct, check that you have designated the correct field on which to calculate the total.

2. In running a group total report, if almost every line has a group total you probably have failed to designate the proper record sequence for the file.

3. If records are not in the desired order in a report, be sure that you selected the correct index.

4. If a character field column is not vertically aligned, you have used [Spacebar] between that field and the preceding field on the report design screen. You can see this because the area between the field definitions will not be shaded. Use [Delete] to delete the spaces. However, fields to the right will be moved left in the process, so you will need to move them back ([F6] to *Select* and [F7] to *Move*) or else delete them and reenter them in their correct positions.

Form Letters and Labels

1. Margins are confusing in mailmerge because each of the detail lines of the initial screen has default margins of 0 and 254. If you change the margins, that change applies only to the line on which the cursor is positioned when you make the change. Always delete all Detail Bands except one, then make your margin changes. That way, all new lines will have the same margin settings (until you make another change).

2. If you want excess spaces between two character fields removed, be sure to create the label form by inserting spaces between the two fields.

Index

NOTES

NOTES